THE WOMAN'S EXCHANGE OF MEMPHIS

Compliments OF

THE WOMAN'S EXCHANGE OF MEMPHIS

Published by The Woman's Exchange of Memphis, Inc.
Copyright © 2006

The Woman's Exchange of Memphis, Inc.
88 Racine Street
Memphis, Tennessee 38111
901.327.2223
901.327.5672 (FAX)
www.womans-exchange.com

Food Styling: Katherine Mistilis, C. E. E.
Food Photography: © E. Wess Bramlitt

ISBN: 0-9760107-0-4

Edited, Designed and Manufactured by Favorite Recipes® Press
An imprint of

FRP

P.O. Box 305142
Nashville, Tennessee 37230
800.358.0560

Art Director: Steve Newman
Book Design: Dave Malone
Project Manager and Editor: Debbie Van Mol, RD

Manufactured in the United States of America
First Printing: 2006   10,000 copies

SPECIAL ACKNOWLEDGMENTS

American Seafood Company • Babcock Galleries • Gift & Art Shop • Gild The Lily
In Bloom • Legacy Linens • Ray & Baudoin

Food Stylist: Katherine Mistilis, C.C.E.
Food Photography: © E. Wess Bramlitt
Titled by: Dixie Wolbrecht

Foreword

"Helping Others To Help Themselves"—a motto invisibly emblazoned on every christening gown, every gooseneck bib, and every Tea Room treat sold at The Woman's Exchange of Memphis.

For seventy-two years, members of The Woman's Exchange, as we know it today, have devoted precious time and energies to fulfilling this motto. The consignors, the seamstresses, and the customers who benefit from the one-of-a-kind treasures sold at the Exchange are as different as roses in a summer garden.

The origins of the Exchange are rooted in the visionary efforts of three Memphis women—Mrs. L. K. Thompson, Mrs. Arthur Halle, and Mrs. David Sternberg. Years ahead of their times, they had the desire to make the mid-South a better and stronger place to dwell.

Originally called The Craft's Exchange, the organization served as an outlet for the needy to market their wares, probably for pennies. Its growth was charged in the 1930s when these three young women and their friends worked in soup kitchens, providing sustenance to the weary. Through the years, wherever the location, whatever the period in history, the goal of the membership of The Woman's Exchange has been to provide a suitable outlet for men and women to display and sell their crafts, and thus enrich life for themselves and their families.

Having previously published three other cookbooks, this fourth culinary endeavor is an extension of that long-cherished motto. All proceeds from sales of this book will allow The Woman's Exchange to continue to extend help to those in need and to better the lives of the deserving. With the passing of time, we live and work by our motto—"Helping Others To Help Themselves."

$\mathcal{T}$able
—OF—
$\mathcal{C}$ontents

CHAPTER 1
Savory Beginnings

CHAPTER 2
Salads & Dressings

CHAPTER 3
Soups & Sandwiches

CHAPTER 4
Brunch & Breads

CHAPTER 5
Meat & Game

5

CHAPTER 9
Just Desserts

9

CHAPTER 6
Seafood & Poultry

6

CHAPTER 7
Pasta & Grains

7

CHAPTER 10
Chefs' Recipes

10

CHAPTER 8
Vegetables & Sides

8

COOKBOOK UNDERWRITERS

The Woman's Exchange of Memphis, Inc., wishes to thank our members and friends whose financial assistance helped to underwrite the publication costs of Compliments of.
Our motto of "Helping Others To Help Themselves" continues to be a reality because of your generosity.

DIAMOND

The Assisi Foundation of Memphis, Inc.

PLATINUM

Peggy and Jim Hughes, Jr.

GOLD

Foy and Bill Coolidge

First Tennessee Foundation

Mickey and Charlie Schaffler

Mary Ann and Robin M. Stevenson, M.D.

The Bridgewater House

Nelse R. Thompson Family

SILVER

A Friend of The Woman's Exchange
Libby and Jack Aaron
Adams Foundation
Athens Distributing Company of
Memphis
Babcock Gifts
Sue and John Dewald
Nancy and Martin Edwards
Equity Inns, Inc.

Farrell Calhoun, Inc.
Sue and Stanley Kaplan, M.D.
King Cotton Chrysler
Bobbie and Bill Lovelace
Morgan Keegan & Company, Inc.
Olympic Industries
Dianne and Larry Papasan
Park Place Hotel

Pediatrics East, Inc.
Roadshow BMW/MINI
Roebuck and Associates
Sandy and Phil Sherman, Jr., D.D.S.
Westonco, Inc.
DixieWolbrecht
Linda and Bill Woodmansee
Woodmansee Wealth Management
Ann and Jim Vining

BRONZE

Carolyn and Peter Carnesale, M.D.
Commercial Bank & Trust Company
Linda and Harry Lee Davidson
Carolyn and John Dobson, M.D.
First American Title Insurance
Company
Emily Roberts Gay
Gorham/Schaffler, Inc.
Carolyn and Tom Grizzard, M.D.

Ann Clark Harris
Lexus of Memphis
Gail and Jack Mitchell
Ginny and Tom Moss
Leslie and Clyde Patton
Prudential Collins-Maury, Inc. Realtors
Carole Horan Pruett
Mary Alice Quinn

Regions Bank
Revenue Assurance Professionals
William W. Schaefer
Susan and Buddy Shindler
Bonnie and Chapman Smith, M.D.
Sovereign Wealth Management, Inc.
Stanford Group Company
The Moran Company
Wittichen Lime and Cement Company

PEWTER

Barbara and Lawrence Adams
Beth and Jim Breazeale
Buster's Liquors and Wines
Judith Campbell
Kitty and Bob Cannon
Jeanne and Al Cash
Sylvia Cochran
Coleman-Etter, Fontaine Realtors
Betty and Alfred Cowles, Jr.
Delta Asset Management
Pattie P. DePriest
Elaine and Tom Edwards
Mary and Tom Elkin, Ph.D.
Jackie and George Falls
Mary Ann and Steve Gammill, M.D.
Graham's Lighting
Renee Clark Guibao
Virginia and Jack Gibson
Jean and Cliff Gorham

Betty and Charles Harbison, D.D.S.
Jo Ann Hardeman
Marcia and Wayland J. Hayes, M.D.
Carol and Al Henderson
Ann and William T. Herring, M.D.
Lunida Holland
Anne and Don Howdeshell
Kellman-Lazarov, Inc.
Ann D. Lansden
JoAnn and Burgess Ledbetter
Mabel and Phil McNeill
Nancy and Rodgers Menzies, Jr.
Mercedes-Benz of Memphis
Barbara and Kelton Morris
Oak Hall
Paragon National Bank
Paulette's
Peter D. Poole Fine Jewelers

William Pruett
Ann Clark Quinlen
Regency Travel, Inc.
RE/MAX on Track
Renasant Bank
Rita Satterfield
SEACAP Financial, Inc.
James E. Sexton, II
Karen Spacek and William Solmson
SPL Corporation
Arthur J. Sutherland, III, M.D.
Sutherland Cardiology Clinic
Diane and Herb Taylor, M.D.
Diana and Joe Teagarden
Barbara and Robert Vincent, M.D.
Barbara and Joseph Walker
Christina Ward
Elise and Bob Wilson
Jane and Lewis Wood

Savory Beginnings

Fried Green Tomatoes with
Red Pepper Rémoulade Sauce *page 12*

Red Pepper Rémoulade Sauce

1/4 cup egg substitute	1 teaspoon lemon juice
1/2 cup vegetable oil	1 garlic clove, minced
1/2 (12-ounce) jar roasted red bell peppers, drained	1/2 teaspoon sugar
1/4 cup minced onion	1/2 teaspoon salt
1 tablespoon Creole mustard	1/2 teaspoon ground cumin
	1/8 teaspoon cayenne pepper

Fried Green Tomatoes

1/2 cup all-purpose flour	2 cups panko (Japanese bread crumbs)
1/2 cup yellow cornmeal	vegetable oil
1/2 teaspoon salt	sprigs of fresh basil or thinly sliced fried onions
1/4 teaspoon pepper	
2 eggs	12 large shrimp, cooked, peeled and deveined (optional)
2 tablespoons water	
3 green tomatoes	

For the sauce, pour the egg substitute into a food processor. Add the oil gradually, processing constantly until thickened. Spoon into a bowl. Combine the roasted bell peppers, onion, Creole mustard, lemon juice, garlic, sugar, salt, cumin and cayenne pepper in the food processor and process until almost smooth but with some texture. Fold the roasted bell pepper mixture into the egg mixture. Chill, covered, in the refrigerator.

For the tomatoes, mix the flour, cornmeal, salt and pepper in a shallow dish. Whisk the eggs and water in a bowl. Cut the tomatoes into twelve 1/8-inch slices and coat with the flour mixture. Dip in the egg mixture and coat with the bread crumbs. Add enough oil to a skillet to measure 1 inch and heat over medium heat. Fry the tomato slices in the hot oil for 2 to 2 1/2 minutes per side; drain. Arrange 3 fried tomato slices on each of 4 serving plates and garnish with sprigs of fresh basil and/or thinly sliced fried onions. Serve with the sauce. Or top each serving with 3 shrimp and drizzle with the sauce.

Photograph for this recipe on page 10.

Crab Cakes with Ravigote Sauce

Ravigote Sauce

1 cup mayonnaise
$1/2$ cup sour cream
2 shallots, minced
4 cornichons, finely chopped
2 tablespoons drained capers, chopped
1 tablespoon white wine vinegar
$1^1/2$ teaspoons minced fresh tarragon
Tabasco sauce to taste

Crab Cakes

$1/4$ cup mayonnaise
1 egg, lightly beaten
2 teaspoons Worcestershire sauce
1 teaspoon Old Bay seasoning
1 teaspoon dry mustard
$1/4$ teaspoon white pepper
1 pound fresh crab meat, drained and
    shells removed
$1/2$ cup cracker crumbs or bread crumbs
cracker crumbs or bread crumbs to coat
vegetable oil

For the sauce, whisk the mayonnaise, sour cream, shallots, pickles, capers, vinegar, tarragon and Tabasco sauce in a bowl until combined. Chill, covered, in the refrigerator.

For the crab cakes, combine the mayonnaise, egg, Worcestershire sauce, Old Bay seasoning, dry mustard and white pepper in a bowl and mix well. Fold in the crab meat and gently stir in $1/2$ cup cracker crumbs.

Shape the crab meat mixture into 6 cakes and coat lightly with cracker crumbs. Sauté the cakes in a small amount of oil in a skillet for 5 minutes per side, turning once. Serve with the sauce.

SAVORY BEGINNINGS

Marinated Shrimp

2 cups thinly sliced red onions
1 1/2 cups canola oil
3/4 cup white vinegar
8 bay leaves
2 1/2 tablespoons undrained capers
2 1/2 teaspoons celery seeds
1 1/2 teaspoons salt
1/8 teaspoon Tabasco sauce
2 1/2 pounds shrimp, cooked, peeled
    and deveined
lettuce

Combine the onions, canola oil, vinegar, bay leaves, capers, celery seeds, salt and Tabasco sauce in a bowl and mix well. Add the shrimp and toss to coat.

Marinate, covered, in the refrigerator for 2 to 10 hours, stirring occasionally. Drain and discard the bay leaves. Serve the shrimp on a bed of lettuce as an appetizer or serve with a baked potato and crusty bread as an entrée.

Coctel de Camarones

6 cups clamato juice
1 1/2 cups pico de gallo
3/4 cup Sprite
1/2 cup fresh cilantro, snipped
1/2 cup chopped onion
1/2 cup chopped celery
1/2 cup chopped seeded tomato
1/4 cup sugar
1/2 large avocado, coarsely chopped
2 teaspoons minced jalapeño
1 tablespoon picante sauce or salsa
32 large shrimp, cooked, peeled and
    deveined
2 limes, cut into quarters
fresh cilantro leaves

Combine the clamato juice, pico de gallo, soda, 1/2 cup cilantro, the onion, celery, tomato, sugar, avocado, jalapeño and picante sauce in a bowl and mix well. Stir in the shrimp. Chill, covered, in the refrigerator. Ladle into soup bowls and serve with the lime wedges and cilantro leaves.

COMPLIMENTS OF

Grilled Oysters with Lemon Dill Sauce

YIELD: 2 TO 4 SERVINGS

1 cup mayonnaise
1/4 cup sour cream or buttermilk
2 tablespoons chopped fresh
    dill weed
1 tablespoon minced fresh parsley
1 tablespoon grated lemon zest
1 tablespoon lemon juice
1 small garlic clove, minced
1/4 teaspoon Tabasco sauce, or
    to taste
1 to 2 dozen unshucked oysters
lemon wedges
clarified butter

Combine the mayonnaise, sour cream, dill weed, parsley, lemon zest, lemon juice, garlic and Tabasco sauce in a bowl and mix well. Chill, covered, in the refrigerator.

Preheat a charcoal or gas grill. Allow the charcoal to burn until white and spread the coals for even heat distribution.

Arrange the oysters curved side down on the grill rack and grill for 5 to 8 minutes or until the shells pop open. Serve immediately with the sauce, along with lemon wedges and/or clarified butter.

Nouveau Quesadillas

YIELD: 8 SERVINGS

Goat Cheese Cream
3 ounces mild goat cheese
4 teaspoons sour cream
2 teaspoons creamy horseradish
2 teaspoons chopped fresh
    dill weed
salt and pepper to taste

Quesadillas
2 (10-inch) flour tortillas
1/4 cup olive oil
1 pound thinly sliced
    smoked salmon
chopped fresh dill weed
sprigs of dill weed

For the cream, mix the goat cheese, sour cream, horseradish, dill weed, salt and pepper in a bowl.

For the quesadillas, preheat the oven to 350 degrees. Sauté the tortillas in the olive oil in a skillet until light brown on both sides; drain. Spread 1 side of each tortilla with some of the cream and layer equally with the salmon. Sprinkle with chopped dill weed.

Arrange the quesadillas on a baking sheet and heat for 5 minutes. Cut into wedges and garnish with sprigs of dill weed. Serve immediately with Champagne. You may prepare in advance and store, covered, in the refrigerator. Heat just before serving.

SAVORY BEGINNINGS

Roquefort Grapes

YIELD: 6 TO 8 SERVINGS

10 ounces walnuts, almonds
    or pecans
8 ounces cream cheese, softened
4 ounces Roquefort or bleu cheese
2 tablespoons heavy cream
1 pound firm seedless red or
    green grapes

Preheat the oven to 275 degrees. Spread the walnuts on a baking sheet and toast until fragrant, stirring occasionally. If using almonds toast until light golden brown in color. Toast pecans until fragrant. Immediately remove the walnuts to a hard surface and coarsely chop.

Combine the cream cheese, Roquefort cheese and heavy cream in a mixing bowl and beat until smooth, scraping the bowl occasionally. Add the grapes to the cream cheese mixture and stir gently to coat.

Roll the coated grapes in the walnuts and arrange in a single layer on a tray lined with waxed paper. Chill until serving time. To serve, arrange the grapes on a platter to resemble a grape cluster and garnish with grapes leaves or ivy. You may freeze any leftover cream cheese mixture for future use.

Tuxedo Potatoes

YIELD: VARIABLE SERVINGS

small unpeeled new potatoes
sour cream
1 small jar caviar, drained
chopped fresh parsley

Combine potatoes with enough water to cover in a saucepan and bring to a boil. Reduce the heat and cook, covered, just until the potatoes are tender. Drain and cool slightly.

Scoop out the center of each potato with a teaspoon or small melon baller and fill the centers with sour cream. Top with a small amount of caviar and sprinkle with parsley. Arrange the potatoes on a serving platter.

COMPLIMENTS OF

Toast Cups
24 slices white sandwich bread, crusts trimmed
olive oil

Mushroom Filling and Assembly
$1/4$ cup ($1/2$ stick) unsalted butter
8 ounces mushrooms, finely chopped
$1/4$ cup finely chopped shallots
2 tablespoons all-purpose flour
1 cup heavy cream
2 tablespoons finely chopped fresh chives
1 tablespoon chopped fresh parsley
1 teaspoon fresh lemon juice
$1/2$ teaspoon kosher salt
$1/8$ to $1/4$ teaspoon cayenne pepper
$1/4$ to $1/2$ teaspoon dried thyme
grated Parmesan cheese
sprigs of fresh thyme

For the cups, preheat the oven to 375 degrees. Flatten the bread slices on a hard surface using a rolling pin. Brush 1 side of each slice with olive oil or spray with nonstick cooking spray. Cut twenty-four 2-inch rounds from the bread slices using a round cutter. Press each round oil side up over the bottom and up the side of a miniature muffin cup and bake for 5 to 7 minutes or until light brown. Remove to a baking sheet to cool. Reduce the oven temperature to 350 degrees.

For the filling, heat the butter in a skillet and add the mushrooms and shallots. Sauté for 10 to 15 minutes or until the mushrooms are tender. Sprinkle the flour over the mushroom mixture and mix well. Stir in the heavy cream and bring just to a boil. Cook until thickened, stirring frequently. Remove from the heat and stir in the chives, parsley, lemon juice, salt, cayenne pepper and dried thyme. Taste and adjust the seasonings.

Spoon the filling into the toast cups and sprinkle with cheese. You may freeze at this point for future use. Bake for 10 minutes or until bubbly. Garnish with sprigs of fresh thyme.

SAVORY BEGINNINGS

Caponata

YIELD: 6¹/₂ CUPS

6 tablespoons olive oil
1 small onion, chopped
1 large rib celery, chopped
1 (14-ounce) can diced tomatoes,
    drained
1 cup canned crushed tomatoes
¹/₂ cup pitted green olives, halved
2 tablespoons red wine vinegar
2 tablespoons drained capers
1 tablespoon sugar
¹/₂ teaspoon salt
¹/₄ teaspoon freshly ground pepper
1 large eggplant, chopped

Heat 2 tablespoons of the olive oil in a saucepan over medium heat. Add the onion and celery to the hot oil and cook, covered, for 10 minutes. Stir in the next 8 ingredients and bring to a boil. Reduce the heat and simmer, covered, for 20 minutes.

Heat 2 tablespoons of the olive oil in a nonstick skillet over medium heat. Add ¹/₂ of the eggplant and cook for 10 minutes or until tender. Remove the eggplant to a bowl using a slotted spoon, reserving the pan drippings.

Heat the remaining 2 tablespoons olive oil with the reserved pan drippings and add the remaining eggplant. Cook for 10 minutes or until tender; drain. Add the eggplant and tomato mixture to the bowl and mix well. Cool and chill. Serve on slices of toasted French bread.

Kalamata Tapenade

YIELD: 1¹/₂ CUPS

1 cup pitted kalamata olives
4 anchovy fillets, drained and rinsed
3 tablespoons drained capers
¹/₂ teaspoon herbes de Provence
2 small garlic cloves
juice of ¹/₂ lemon, or to taste
freshly ground pepper to taste
¹/₄ cup olive oil

Combine the olives, anchovies, capers, herbes de Provence, garlic, lemon juice and pepper in a food processor and process until coarsely chopped. Add the olive oil gradually, processing constantly until the consistency of a coarse purée. Chill, covered, in the refrigerator. Serve chilled or at room temperature with assorted party crackers.

COMPLIMENTS OF

Bleu Cheese Dip with Apples and Pears

YIELD: 8 (OR MORE) SERVINGS

1 or 2 unpeeled Granny
    Smith apples
1 or 2 unpeeled pears
orange juice
1 cup commercially prepared
    bleu cheese salad dressing
8 ounces cream cheese, softened
4 ounces bleu cheese, crumbled
1 cup pecan pieces, toasted

Slice the apples and pears and place in a bowl. Pour enough orange juice over the fruit to cover in order to prevent browning and store, covered, in the refrigerator.

Combine the salad dressing and cream cheese in a mixing bowl and beat until blended. Stir in the bleu cheese and pecans. Spoon the dip into a small bowl and place in the center of a platter. Drain the fruit and arrange around the dip.

Hot Crab and Artichoke Dip

YIELD: 5 CUPS

1 cup (2 sticks) unsalted butter
1 small onion, finely chopped
3 or 4 garlic cloves, minced
1 cup all-purpose flour
10 green onions, finely chopped
1 quart half-and-half
2 pounds lump crab meat, drained
    and shells removed
2 (14-ounce) cans artichoke hearts,
    drained and coarsely chopped
$1/2$ cup white wine
salt and pepper to taste

Heat the butter in a heavy saucepan and add the chopped onion and garlic. Sauté for 5 minutes or until the onion is tender. Add the flour gradually and cook until a roux forms, stirring constantly. Add the green onions and cook for 1 to 2 minutes.

Add the half-and-half and cook until the mixture begins to thicken, stirring constantly. Add the crab meat, artichokes, wine, salt and pepper and cook just until heated through, stirring frequently. Serve hot with assorted party crackers.

EASY PEPPER JELLY

Combine 1/2 cup apple jelly, 1/2 cup orange marmalade, 1 tablespoon chopped seeded jalapeño chile, 1 tablespoon finely chopped onion and 1 teaspoon cider vinegar in a saucepan and mix well. Cook over low heat until the jelly and marmalade melt, stirring frequently. Chill, covered, for 8 hours. Serve over cream cheese with assorted party crackers.

2 cups chopped onions
2 garlic cloves, minced
2 tablespoons butter
2 pounds white Cheddar cheese, shredded
1 to 2 cups heavy cream
4 tomatoes, seeded and chopped
1 (4-ounce) can chopped hot green chiles, drained
1 poblano chile, chopped

Sauté the onions and garlic in the butter in a skillet until the onions are tender. Heat the cheese in a double boiler over hot water until melted, stirring occasionally. Stir in the heavy cream. Add the onion mixture, tomatoes, green chiles and poblano chile to the cheese mixture and simmer just until heated through, stirring frequently.

Spoon the queso into a fondue pot and serve hot with crusty bread chunks, fresh vegetables and/or boiled new potatoes.

Mexican Guacamole

YIELD: 1¹/₂ CUPS

¹/₄ onion, coarsely chopped
2 garlic cloves
1 or 2 canned jalapeños
    with juice
5 or 6 sprigs of cilantro
3 avocados, chopped
juice of 1 lime, or to taste
salt to taste
chopped fresh tomato

Combine the onion, garlic, jalapeños and cilantro in a food processor and process until finely chopped. Add the avocados and lime juice and process until smooth. Season to taste with salt. Chill, covered, in the refrigerator.

Spoon the guacamole into a bowl and garnish with chopped tomato. Serve with tortilla chips.

Ranchero Salsa

YIELD: 6 TO 8 SERVINGS

1 (16-ounce) can yellow corn,
    drained
1 (16-ounce) can black beans,
    drained
4 tomatoes, chopped
1¹/₄ cups chopped fresh cilantro
1 bunch green onions, chopped
1 green bell pepper, chopped
1 avocado, coarsely chopped
¹/₄ cup fresh lime juice
¹/₂ to 1 jalapeño, chopped
1 tablespoon ground cumin
¹/₄ teaspoon salt

Combine the corn, beans, tomatoes, cilantro, green onions, bell pepper, avocado, lime juice, jalapeño, cumin and salt in a bowl and mix gently. Let stand, covered, for 3 to 4 hours before serving. Serve with corn chips.

SAVORY BEGINNINGS

YIELD: 1³/4 CUPS

COCKTAIL CHERRY TOMATOES

Lightly coat cherry tomatoes with olive oil and sprinkle with kosher salt. Chill and serve with wooden picks.

Cocktail Cherry Tomatoes, Sausage Scoops (page 28), and Mexican Guacamole with tortilla chips (page 21) make a nice array of hors d'oeuvre before dinner with friends.

1 cup mayonnaise or light
  mayonnaise
¹/2 cup sour cream or
  light sour cream
¹/2 cup chopped fresh basil
1 tablespoon tomato paste
1 tablespoon grated lemon zest
1 garlic clove, crushed
¹/2 teaspoon Worcestershire sauce

Combine the mayonnaise, sour cream, basil, tomato paste, lemon zest, garlic and Worcestershire sauce in a bowl and mix well. Chill, covered, for up to 2 days. Serve with chips or raw vegetables.

*Sharing a recipe is
a way of extending your life.*

Dill Dip

YIELD: 1 1/3 CUPS

2/3 cup mayonnaise
2/3 cup sour cream
1 tablespoon finely sliced green
    onion
1 tablespoon parsley flakes
1 teaspoon dill weed
1 teaspoon seasoned salt

Combine the mayonnaise, sour cream, green onion, parsley flakes, dill weed and seasoned salt in a bowl and mix well. Chill, covered, in the refrigerator. Serve with assorted chips and/or chunks of raw vegetables.

It's Greek to Me Dip

YIELD: 2 CUPS

1 cup mayonnaise or light
    mayonnaise
1/2 cup crumbled feta cheese or
    seasoned feta cheese
1/2 cup sour cream or light
    sour cream
10 pickled pepperoncini, stems
    removed
3 to 5 large garlic cloves, chopped
3 tablespoons drained small capers
2 tablespoons parsley flakes, or an
    equivalent amount of chopped
    fresh parsley
2 teaspoons lemon juice
1 1/2 teaspoons oregano
1 teaspoon freshly ground pepper
1/2 teaspoon Tabasco sauce, or
    to taste
chopped fresh chives or paprika

Combine the mayonnaise, cheese, sour cream, pepperoncini, garlic and capers in a food processor. Add the parsley flakes, lemon juice, oregano, pepper and Tabasco sauce and process until blended but with some texture.

Spoon the dip into a bowl and sprinkle with chopped fresh chives. Surround with raw vegetables, pita crisps and/or pita chips. Or scoop out the centers of cherry tomatoes and fill the centers with the dip.

Caramelized Onion and Basil Spread

YIELD: 8 SERVINGS

2 tablespoons extra-virgin olive oil
1 large Spanish onion,
    finely chopped
1 tablespoon balsamic vinegar
8 ounces cream cheese, softened
3 tablespoons finely shredded fresh
    basil leaves
1/4 teaspoon seasoned salt
6 to 8 grinds of black pepper
1/8 teaspoon hot red pepper sauce

Heat the olive oil in a nonstick skillet over medium-low heat. Add the onion to the hot oil and cook until tender and just beginning to brown, stirring occasionally. Stir in the vinegar and cook until most of the liquid evaporates, stirring occasionally. Remove from the heat and let stand until cool.

Combine the cooled onion mixture, cream cheese and basil in a bowl and mix well. Stir in the salt, black pepper and hot red pepper sauce. Serve with assorted party crackers and/or party bread.

Beale Street Log

YIELD: 8 SERVINGS

8 ounces cream cheese or light
    cream cheese, softened
1 tablespoon grated onion
1/2 garlic clove, minced
1/2 teaspoon dill weed
1 cup pecans, chopped and toasted
1/4 cup (1/2 stick) butter
1/4 cup packed dark brown sugar
1 teaspoon Worcestershire sauce
1/2 teaspoon prepared
    yellow mustard

Combine the cream cheese, onion, garlic and dill weed in a bowl and mix well. Shape the cream cheese mixture into a log and wrap with waxed paper. Chill for 8 to 10 hours.

Combine the pecans, butter, brown sugar, Worcestershire sauce and prepared mustard in a saucepan. Bring to a boil and boil until the brown sugar dissolves, stirring frequently. Let stand until cool and spoon over the cheese log on a serving platter. Serve with wheat crackers.

COMPLIMENTS OF

Holiday Cheese

YIELD: 12 TO 16 SERVINGS

1 (4-ounce) jar diced pimentos, drained
1/2 cup olive oil
1/2 cup white wine vinegar
3 tablespoons chopped fresh parsley
3 tablespoons minced green onions
3 garlic cloves, minced
1 teaspoon sugar
3/4 teaspoon dried basil, or an equivalent amount
    of fresh basil
1/2 teaspoon salt
1/2 teaspoon freshly ground pepper
1 (8-ounce) block sharp Cheddar cheese, chilled
1 (8-ounce) block cream cheese, chilled
sprigs of parsley

Combine the pimentos, olive oil, vinegar, chopped parsley, green onions, garlic, sugar, basil, salt and pepper in a jar with a tight-fitting lid and seal tightly. Shake to mix.

Cut the Cheddar cheese block lengthwise into halves. Cut each half into 1/4-inch slices. Repeat the process with the cream cheese. Arrange the cheese slices alternately in a shallow dish and pour the olive oil mixture over the cheese. Marinate, covered, in the refrigerator for 8 hours or longer.

To serve, arrange the slices in the same alternating pattern on a serving platter. Spoon the marinade over the cheese and serve with assorted party crackers. Garnish with sprigs of parsley.

SAVORY BEGINNINGS

Summer Trees is the name of a beautiful antebellum home located in Mississippi. It has been the site of many lovely parties. Two verandas surround the home. Here, guests often gather to celebrate special occasions. These mushrooms are a favorite, whether served at brunch, luncheons, or dinner parties.

YIELD: 4 DOZEN MUSHROOMS

2 pounds medium mushrooms
16 ounces cream cheese, softened
1 envelope ranch party dip mix
$^1/_2$ cup (2 ounces) grated
    Parmesan cheese
$^1/_4$ cup mayonnaise
2 tablespoons minced green onions
1 tablespoon chopped fresh
    parsley
1 cup herb-seasoned stuffing mix,
    crushed
$^1/_2$ cup (1 stick) butter, melted
chopped fresh parsley

Preheat the oven to 350 degrees. Remove the stems from the mushrooms. Combine the cream cheese, dip mix, Parmesan cheese, mayonnaise, green onions and parsley in a bowl and mix well.

Mound some of the cream cheese mixture in each mushroom cap. Turn the stuffed mushrooms over and dip in the stuffing mix. Arrange the mushrooms stuffing side up in two 9×13-inch baking dishes and drizzle with the butter. Bake for 30 minutes and sprinkle with parsley.

Mushroom caps may be baked in advance. Arrange the caps stem side down on a wire rack over a baking sheet and bake at 325 degrees for 5 minutes. Stuff with the desired filling and bake.

SMOKED SALMON
PINWHEELS

Spread Goat Cheese Cream

(page 15) on slices of

smoked salmon and roll.

Slice the rolls into pinwheels

and arrange the slices on

pumpernickel rounds.

Garnish with sprigs of

dill weed.

COMPLIMENTS OF

Monterey Jack Pie

YIELD: 10 TO 12 SERVINGS

2 refrigerator pie pastries
2 pounds Monterey Jack cheese,
    thinly sliced
1 (14-ounce) jar apricot preserves
milk or an egg wash (optional)

Preheat the oven to 425 degrees. Line a quiche pan with 1 of the pastries. Layer the cheese evenly over the pastry and spread with the preserves. Top with the remaining pastry, sealing the edge and cutting vents. Brush with milk or an egg wash.

Bake for 20 minutes. Cut the pie into 6 wedges; do not remove the wedges from the pan. Place the pan on a trivet or in a chafing dish. Serve with assorted party crackers and/or sliced Granny Smith apples.

Bleu Cheese Puffs

YIELD: 50 TO 60 PUFFS

16 ounces cream cheese, softened
1 cup mayonnaise or light
    mayonnaise
3 to 4 ounces bleu cheese, crumbled
1 tablespoon minced onion
$1/4$ cup minced fresh chives or green
    onion tops
$1/2$ teaspoon (scant) cayenne pepper
2 loaves thinly sliced firm
    white bread
paprika

Combine the cream cheese and mayonnaise in a bowl and mix well. Stir in the bleu cheese, onion, chives and cayenne pepper.

Cut the bread into $1^1/2$- to 2-inch rounds using a round cutter. Spread 1 tablespoon of the cream cheese mixture on each round. Arrange the rounds in a single layer on a baking sheet and freeze, covered, until firm.

Preheat the oven to 350 degrees. Bake for 15 to 25 minutes or until brown and bubbly. Sprinkle with paprika and serve immediately.

SAVORY BEGINNINGS

27

Sausage Scoops

YIELD: 6 DOZEN SCOOPS

1 pound country sausage
1^1/$_2$ cups (6 ounces) shredded mild
    Cheddar cheese
1^1/$_2$ cups (6 ounces) shredded
    Mexican Jack cheese
^{2}/$_3$ cup ranch salad dressing
1 (6-ounce) can pitted black olives,
    drained and chopped
^{1}/$_2$ cup chopped fresh cilantro
1 red bell pepper, chopped
1 jalapeño, minced
cayenne pepper to taste
tortilla scoops
sliced black olives
fresh herbs

Preheat the oven to 350 degrees. Brown the sausage in a skillet and drain. Cool slightly and crumble into a bowl. Add the Cheddar cheese, Mexican Jack cheese, salad dressing, chopped olives, cilantro, bell pepper, jalapeño and cayenne pepper to the sausage and mix well. You may freeze, covered, at this point for future use.

Spoon 1 tablespoon of the sausage mixture into each tortilla scoop and arrange on a baking sheet. Bake for 5 to 8 minutes or until heated through. Top each scoop with an olive slice and garnish with fresh herbs.

Pita Cheese Crisps

YIELD: 5 DOZEN CRISPS

4 cups (16 ounces) finely shredded
    sharp Cheddar cheese
1^3/$_4$ cups (3^1/$_2$ sticks) unsalted
    butter, softened
^{2}/$_3$ cup freshly grated
    Romano cheese
^{3}/$_4$ teaspoon Worcestershire sauce
1 garlic clove, minced
1 teaspoon paprika
^{1}/$_4$ teaspoon cayenne pepper
6 pita bread rounds, split

Preheat the oven to 350 degrees. Combine the Cheddar cheese, butter, Romano cheese, Worcestershire sauce, garlic, paprika and cayenne pepper in a bowl and mix well.

Spread the cheese mixture on 1 side of each pita round and cut each round into 5 wedges. Arrange the wedges in a single layer on a baking sheet and bake for 12 minutes or until brown and crisp. Serve with cocktails or as an accompaniment to soups or salads.

COMPLIMENTS OF

Smoked Catfish

YIELD: 48 SERVINGS

Garlic Butter Sauce
1/2 cup (1 stick) butter
1/2 cup extra-virgin olive oil
1 teaspoon granulated garlic

Catfish
4 whole catfish, dressed
freshly ground pepper
poultry seasoning
Old Bay seasoning
red leaf lettuce

For the sauce, melt the butter in a saucepan. Stir in the olive oil and garlic and cook until heated though, stirring occasionally.

For the catfish, preheat a smoker with a water pan. Pat the catfish dry with paper towels and rub heavily with pepper. Mix equal parts of poultry seasoning and Old Bay seasoning in a bowl and rub over the surfaces of the catfish. Spray the smoker rack with nonstick cooking spray and arrange the catfish on the rack.

Smoke for 1 hour, then baste the top sides of the catfish with some of the sauce. Smoke for 3 hours longer, basting the top sides with the sauce every 45 minutes. Arrange the catfish on an oval serving platter lined with red leaf lettuce and serve warm with saltine crackers.

Crawfish Delight

YIELD: 4 CUPS

1/4 cup (1/2 stick) butter
6 green onions, chopped
4 garlic cloves, crushed
1 pound crawfish tails, chopped
12 ounces cream cheese or fat-free cream cheese, cubed
1/2 teaspoon cracked black pepper
1/2 teaspoon garlic salt
1/8 teaspoon red pepper, or to taste

Melt the butter in a saucepan and add the green onions and garlic. Sauté until the green onions are tender. Stir in the crawfish tails and cream cheese and cook until the cream cheese melts, stirring frequently. Stir in the black pepper, garlic salt and red pepper. Spoon the crawfish mixture into a chafing dish and serve warm with assorted party crackers.

SAVORY BEGINNINGS

Salads
&
Dressings

Mosaic Salad *page 41*

YIELD: 4 SERVINGS

FRENCH VINAIGRETTE

Whisk 3 tablespoons white wine vinegar, 1 teaspoon Dijon mustard, 1/2 teaspoon salt, 1/8 teaspoon pepper and 2 teaspoons finely chopped shallot in a bowl until mixed. Add 6 tablespoons extra-virgin olive oil gradually, whisking constantly until incorporated. Use as an alternative for Lemon Vinaigrette.

Lemon Vinaigrette
2 teaspoons fresh lemon juice
2 teaspoons white wine vinegar
1/4 teaspoon grated lemon zest
sea salt and freshly ground pepper
to taste
1/4 cup olive oil

Salad
watercress or mixed salad greens
endive spears
1 pear or apple, cut into
16 thin slices
4 slices goat cheese
toasted crushed pecans or walnuts
plumped currants

For the vinaigrette, whisk the lemon juice, vinegar, lemon zest, salt and pepper in a bowl. Add the olive oil gradually, whisking constantly until incorporated.

For the salad, toss the watercress with the Lemon Vinaigrette or French Vinaigrette (sidebar) in a bowl until coated. Fan the endive spears around the edges of 4 salad plates and fill the centers of the plates with equal portions of the dressed watercress.

Preheat the broiler. Fan out 4 slices of the pear on a baking sheet and top with 1 slice of the goat cheese. Repeat the process with the remaining pear slices and goat cheese. Broil until bubbly and arrange over the salads. Sprinkle with the pecans and currants and serve immediately.

Watermelon Salad

YIELD: 12 SERVINGS

Champagne Vinaigrette
1/4 cup olive oil
2 tablespoons Champagne vinegar

Salad
8 cups watermelon chunks, seeded
1 bunch green onions,
    finely chopped
1/4 cup chopped fresh mint
1 jalapeño, minced
sprigs of mint

For the vinaigrette, whisk the olive oil and vinegar in a bowl until incorporated.

For the salad, toss the watermelon, green onions, chopped mint and jalapeño in a bowl. Add 1/2 of the vinaigrette and toss gently to coat.

Spoon the salad into a glass or silver bowl and garnish with sprigs of mint. You may prepare the salad in advance and store, covered, in the refrigerator.

Frosty Grape Salad

YIELD: 10 TO 12 SERVINGS

1 pound walnuts or pecans
1 cup sour cream
8 ounces cream cheese, softened
1 teaspoon vanilla extract
2 pounds seedless red grapes
2 pounds seedless green grapes
1 cup packed brown sugar

Preheat the oven to 375 degrees. Spread the walnuts in a single layer on a baking sheet and toast until fragrant. Cool and chop. Beat the sour cream, cream cheese and vanilla in a mixing bowl until smooth.

Combine the sour cream mixture and grapes in a bowl and toss to coat. Mix the brown sugar and walnuts together and spread over the grape mixture. Chill, covered, for 1 hour or longer. Serve very cold.

SALADS & DRESSINGS

Confetti Fruit Slaw

ITALIAN VINAIGRETTE

Whisk 2 tablespoons red wine vinegar, 1/2 teaspoon salt and 1/8 teaspoon pepper in a bowl. Add 5 tablespoons extra-virgin olive oil gradually, whisking constantly until incorporated. Drizzle over shredded cabbage or mixed salad greens.

5 cups chopped cabbage
2 apples, chopped
sections of 2 oranges, chopped
1 cup grapes
1/2 cup whipping cream
1 tablespoon sugar
3/4 cup chopped pecans
1/2 cup mayonnaise
1 tablespoon lemon juice
1/2 teaspoon (or more)
   curry powder
1/4 teaspoon salt
paprika or fresh mint

Combine the cabbage, apples, oranges and grapes in a bowl and mix well. Beat the whipping cream in a mixing bowl until soft peaks form. Add the sugar and mix well.

Mix the pecans, mayonnaise, lemon juice, curry powder and salt in a bowl and fold into the whipped cream. Fold the whipped cream mixture into the cabbage mixture and chill, covered, in the refrigerator. Sprinkle with paprika or garnish with fresh mint before serving.

4 chicken breasts
1/4 cup chopped onion
2 ribs celery
1/2 teaspoon peppercorns
1/2 teaspoon salt
1 bay leaf
1/4 teaspoon ground cloves
1 cup mayonnaise
1 cup sliced pimento-stuffed green olives
2 tablespoons grated onion
1 tablespoon tarragon
1 teaspoon Worcestershire sauce
1 teaspoon lemon juice
1/2 teaspoon curry powder (optional)
1/2 teaspoon dry mustard
1/4 teaspoon cayenne pepper
lettuce or fresh tomato shells

Combine the chicken, chopped onion, celery, peppercorns, salt, bay leaf and cloves in a stockpot. Bring to a boil and reduce the heat to low. Simmer for 20 minutes. Remove from the heat and let the chicken stand in the stock until cool. Remove the chicken and chop, discarding the skin and bones. The chopped chicken should measure about 4 cups.

Mix the mayonnaise, olives, grated onion, tarragon, Worcestershire sauce, lemon juice, curry powder, dry mustard and cayenne pepper in a bowl. Add the chicken to the mayonnaise mixture and mix well. Chill, covered, until serving time. To serve, spoon the chicken salad onto a lettuce-lined platter or spoon into fresh tomato shells. Serve with fresh fruit.

SALADS & DRESSINGS

Orange Crab Salad

YIELD: 4 SERVINGS

Red Wine Dressing
6 tablespoons extra-virgin olive oil
2 tablespoons red wine vinegar
juice of $1/2$ lemon
1 tablespoon chopped fresh parsley
2 sprigs of oregano, leaves stripped
    and chopped

Salad
1 pint fresh crab meat, drained and
    shells removed
sections of 2 oranges, chopped
$1/2$ small red onion, thinly sliced
4 Boston or butter lettuce cups
1 avocado, sliced
lemon juice

For the dressing, whisk the olive oil,
vinegar, lemon juice, parsley and oregano
in a bowl until incorporated.

For the salad, toss the crab meat, oranges
and onion in a bowl. Drizzle the dressing
over the crab meat mixture and toss lightly.
Spoon the salad evenly into the lettuce cups
on salad plates. Garnish each salad with
avocado slices dipped in lemon juice.

Shrimp and Mango Salad

YIELD: 2 SERVINGS

$1/4$ cup mayonnaise
2 teaspoons prepared horseradish
1 tablespoon white vinegar
$1/8$ teaspoon pepper
12 ounces peeled cooked shrimp
1 cup chopped fresh mango
$3/4$ cup cooked rice
$1/4$ cup chopped red bell pepper
$1/4$ cup chopped green bell pepper
    (optional)
sprigs of parsley or basil

Combine the mayonnaise, horseradish,
vinegar and pepper in a bowl and whisk
until combined. Stir in the shrimp, mango,
rice and bell peppers. Chill, covered, in
the refrigerator.

Spoon the salad onto lettuce-lined salad
plates and garnish with sprigs of parsley or
basil. Serve with crusty French bread and a
glass of wine.

Shrimp Mousse

YIELD: 12 TO 15 SERVINGS

16 ounces cream cheese or light cream cheese, softened
2 cups sour cream or light sour cream
1 cup mayonnaise or light mayonnaise
2 tablespoons unflavored gelatin
1/4 cup cold water
juice of 2 lemons
1/2 cup finely chopped bell pepper
1/2 cup finely chopped green onions
1/4 cup finely chopped pimentos
2 ribs celery, finely chopped
1/2 cup chili sauce
1 teaspoon salt
1 teaspoon Worcestershire sauce
1/8 teaspoon Tabasco sauce
4 to 6 cups chopped peeled cooked shrimp
lemon wedges
sprigs of parsley

Combine the cream cheese, sour cream and mayonnaise in a mixing bowl and beat until creamy, scraping the bowl occasionally. Soften the gelatin in a mixture of the cold water and lemon juice in a bowl. Heat the gelatin mixture in a double boiler for 5 to 10 minutes or until the gelatin dissolves, stirring occasionally.

Fold the gelatin mixture into the cream cheese mixture. Stir in the bell pepper, green onions, pimentos, celery, chili sauce, salt, Worcestershire sauce and Tabasco sauce. Add the shrimp and mix well.

Spoon the shrimp mixture into a greased 8- to 10-cup ring mold or bundt pan. Chill for 8 hours or longer. To serve, dip the mold in warm water for 30 seconds and invert the mousse onto a lettuce-lined platter. Return the mousse to the refrigerator for several minutes to firm the side. Garnish with lemon wedges and sprigs of parsley. Or spoon the shrimp mixture into a 9×13-inch dish sprayed with nonstick cooking spray and chill until set. Cut into squares to serve.

ARTICHOKE DRESSING

Combine 10 tablespoons canola oil, 6 tablespoons tarragon vinegar, 2 tablespoons water, 1 teaspoon salt, 1/2 teaspoon pepper, 1/4 teaspoon onion powder, 1/4 teaspoon garlic powder, 1/2 teaspoon parsley flakes, and one 14-ounce can chopped drained artichokes in a quart jar. Cover the jar and shake to combine. Serve over mixed salad greens.

Mixed Greens with

Raspberry Vinaigrette

YIELD: 8 TO 10 SERVINGS

Raspberry Vinaigrette
1/2 cup sugar
1/2 cup vegetable oil
1/2 cup raspberry vinegar
1/4 cup chopped shallots
2 teaspoons raspberry jam

Salad
2 heads Bibb lettuce, separated
   into leaves
1 bunch red leaf lettuce, separated
   into leaves
1 to 1 1/2 cups seedless red
   grape halves
8 ounces Monterey Jack cheese,
   cubed
1 cup pecans, toasted and
   chopped

For the vinaigrette, whisk the sugar, oil, vinegar, shallots and jam in a bowl until incorporated. Prepare 1 day in advance and store, covered, at room temperature.

For the salad, mix the Bibb lettuce, red leaf lettuce, grapes, cheese and pecans in a salad bowl. Add the desired amount of vinaigrette and toss to coat.

COMPLIMENTS OF

YIELD: 1 SERVING

Creole Rémoulade Sauce

6 tablespoons olive oil

1/4 cup Creole mustard

2 tablespoons vinegar

1 1/2 teaspoons paprika

1/2 teaspoon salt

1/2 teaspoon white pepper

1/4 cup finely chopped celery

1/4 cup finely chopped onion

2 tablespoons finely chopped
    fresh parsley

Basil Vinaigrette

1/4 cup white wine vinegar

1 tablespoon Dijon mustard

2 teaspoons minced shallot

1/2 cup basil-flavored olive oil

kosher salt and freshly ground
    pepper to taste

Salad

1/4 cup crawfish tails

3 peeled cooked large shrimp

1 1/2 cups arugula

3 grape tomatoes

1/2 avocado, sliced

5 kalamata olives

8 haricots verts or thin green
    beans, cooked

For the sauce, whisk the olive oil, Creole mustard, vinegar, paprika, salt and white pepper in a bowl until blended. Stir in the celery, onion and parsley. Chill, covered, for 2 hours.

For the vinaigrette, combine the vinegar, Dijon mustard and shallot in a bowl and mix well. Add the olive oil gradually, whisking constantly until incorporated. Season to taste with salt and pepper.

For the salad, toss the crawfish and shrimp with some of the sauce in a bowl and drain. Arrange the crawfish mixture on a bed of arugula on a serving plate and garnish with the grape tomatoes, avocado, olives and haricots verts. Drizzle lightly with the vinaigrette.

39

Emerald Isle Salad

YIELD: 4 TO 6 SERVINGS

1 cup cubed potato
1 pound green beans, trimmed
3 tablespoons olive oil
1 tablespoon red wine vinegar
1/4 teaspoon salt
1/4 teaspoon freshly ground pepper
1/3 cup (or less) mayonnaise
2 hard-cooked eggs, chopped
3 tablespoons minced fresh parsley
1 tablespoon minced shallot or
    green onion
1 tablespoon Dijon mustard
cherry tomatoes, cut into halves

Combine the potato with enough water to cover in a saucepan and cook until tender; drain. Cover to keep warm. Combine the beans with enough water to cover in a saucepan and cook until tender-crisp; drain. Cover to keep warm.

Whisk the olive oil, vinegar, salt and pepper in a bowl. Add the warm potato and warm beans to the olive oil mixture and toss to coat. Chill, covered, in the refrigerator.

Combine the mayonnaise, eggs, parsley, shallot and Dijon mustard in a bowl and mix well. Add the mayonnaise mixture to the chilled potato mixture and mix gently. Garnish with cherry tomato halves.

Caprese Brochette

YIELD: VARIABLE SERVINGS

grape or cherry tomatoes
basil leaves
marinated bocconcini
olive oil (optional)

Alternate tomatoes, basil and cheese on 6-inch wooden skewers. Drizzle lightly with olive oil just before serving.

…, and above all, have a good time.
Bon Appétit!

—Julia Child, America's Favorite Chef

COMPLIMENTS OF

Mosaic Salad

YIELD: 4 SERVINGS

1 red beet, trimmed
1 yellow beet, trimmed
1 orange beet, trimmed
1 tablespoon red wine vinegar
1½ teaspoons balsamic vinegar
kosher salt and freshly ground
    pepper to taste
¼ cup extra-virgin olive oil
3 tablespoons minced fresh basil
1 head Boston lettuce, separated
1 yellow or red tomato, cut into
    4 slices
8 ounces chèvre, crumbled
edible flowers (optional)

Combine the beets with enough water to cover in a saucepan and cook for 30 to 60 minutes or until tender. Drain and cool slightly. Peel and cut each beet horizontally into 4 slices. Whisk the red wine vinegar, balsamic vinegar, salt and pepper in a bowl. Add the olive oil gradually, whisking constantly until incorporated. Add the basil. Toss the lettuce with the vinaigrette in a bowl.

Mound equal portions of the dressed lettuce on each of 4 salad plates. Arrange 1 slice of each color beet and 1 tomato slice on each plate in a decorative fashion and sprinkle with the cheese. Garnish with edible flowers.

Photograph for this recipe on page 30.

Tomato-Tomato Salad

YIELD: 12 SERVINGS

6 large pieces oil-pack sun-dried
    tomatoes
½ cup fresh basil
¼ cup olive oil
2 tablespoons red wine vinegar
1 tablespoon chopped onion
salt and pepper to taste
2 tablespoons drained capers
8 to 10 large summer tomatoes,
    sliced
fresh basil leaves

Combine the sun-dried tomatoes, ½ cup basil, the olive oil, vinegar and onion in a food processor and process until blended. Season to taste with salt and pepper and stir in the capers.

Arrange the sliced tomatoes on a serving platter and surround with fresh basil leaves. Drizzle with the sun-dried tomato dressing and serve immediately.

A delicious and impressive salad served with Forgotten Beef Tenderloin (page 94), Roasted Shallots (page 176), and Almond Tuile with Lemon Ice Cream (page 180).

2 cups sugar
$^1/_2$ cup water
4 basil leaves
3 tarragon leaves
$1^1/_2$ cups Champagne vinegar
$^1/_2$ cup (1 stick) butter, sliced
$1^1/_2$ cups extra-virgin olive oil
salt and pepper to taste
10 tablespoons extra-virgin
    olive oil
6 tomatoes, cut into $^3/_8$-inch slices
sea salt to taste
10 ounces goat cheese, sliced into
    1-ounce rounds
20 rounds Sally Lunn bread
mixed salad greens

Combine the sugar and water in a saucepan and bring to a boil. Stir in the basil and tarragon and boil until the syrup begins to color. Reduce the heat to low and simmer until the syrup is deep amber in color. Remove from the heat and stir in the vinegar. Cool slightly and whisk in the butter until blended. Place the saucepan over a bowl of ice and whisk in $1^1/_2$ cups olive oil until incorporated. Season to taste with salt and pepper.

Preheat the oven to 375 degrees. Coat 10 ramekins with some of the 10 tablespoons olive oil. Press 1 tomato slice into each prepared ramekin until the tomato completely covers the bottom and sprinkle with sea salt and pepper. Flatten the cheese slices and arrange over the tomato slices. Top each with 1 bread round. Repeat the layering process, omitting the cheese and ending with the bread rounds. Brush the bread rounds with the remaining olive oil and bake for 5 to 6 minutes. Let stand for 2 minutes and invert onto individual salad plates lined with salad greens. Drizzle with the sauce and serve.

COMPLIMENTS OF

Panzanella

YIELD: 8 TO 10 SERVINGS

8 cups dry Italian or French
    bread cubes
3 tomatoes, seeded and chopped
1¹/₂ cups kalamata olives,
    cut into halves
¹/₂ cup fresh basil leaves
1 small red onion, cut into halves
    and thinly sliced
1 cucumber, peeled, seeded and
    chopped
2 ribs celery, chopped
3 garlic cloves, minced
¹/₄ cup extra-virgin olive oil
2 tablespoons red wine vinegar
sea salt and freshly ground pepper
    to taste
basil chiffonade

Toss the bread cubes, tomatoes, olives, basil leaves, onion, cucumber, celery and garlic in a large salad bowl. Whisk the olive oil and vinegar in a bowl until blended and drizzle over the bread mixture 30 minutes before serving. Season to taste with salt and pepper and garnish with basil chiffonade. Makes a great vegetarian entrée.

Corn Bread Salad

YIELD: 12 SERVINGS

1 envelope buttermilk-ranch salad
    dressing mix
12 cups crumbled corn bread
1 pound sliced bacon, crisp-cooked
    and crumbled
1 bunch green onions, chopped
1 (15-ounce) can Shoe Peg corn,
    drained
2¹/₂ cups (10 ounces) shredded
    sharp Cheddar cheese
3 tomatoes, peeled, seeded and
    chopped
2 or 3 hard-cooked eggs, chopped
    (optional)

Prepare the salad dressing mix using the package directions 1 day in advance. Store, covered, in the refrigerator.

Combine the corn bread, bacon, green onions, corn, cheese, tomatoes and eggs in a bowl and mix gently. Add the salad dressing and toss to coat. Chill, covered, for 1¹/₂ hours or longer before serving.

Avocado Dressing

YIELD: 2 CUPS

1 1/2 cups mayonnaise
1 ripe avocado, mashed
1/4 cup heavy cream
juice of 1 lemon
1 garlic clove, minced
1 teaspoon salt
1/2 teaspoon anchovy paste
1/4 teaspoon freshly ground pepper

Combine the mayonnaise, avocado, heavy cream and lemon juice in a bowl and mix well. Stir in the garlic, salt, anchovy paste and pepper. Store, covered, in the refrigerator.

Accelerate the ripening process of an avocado by placing it in a brown paper bag with a banana. The avocado will ripen in about 24 hours. If the avocado is not too hard, place in a bowl and cover with cornmeal. Allow about 8 hours for this process.

Citrus Salad Dressing

YIELD: 1/2 CUP

4 teaspoons Dijon mustard
4 teaspoons orange juice
2 teaspoons white vinegar
salt and pepper to taste
1/4 cup olive oil

Whisk the Dijon mustard, orange juice, vinegar, salt and pepper in a bowl. Add the olive oil gradually, whisking constantly until incorporated. Drizzle over mesclun or spinach tossed with assorted citrus fruit sections.

COMPLIMENTS OF

Parmesan Dressing

YIELD: 2 CUPS

3/4 cup (3 ounces) grated
    Parmesan cheese
1/2 cup sour cream
1/2 cup mayonnaise
1/4 cup balsamic Italian
    salad dressing
1/2 teaspoon cracked pepper

Whisk the cheese, sour cream, mayonnaise, Italian dressing and pepper in a bowl until combined. Serve over your favorite mixed salad greens. Store, covered, in the refrigerator.

To improve the flavor of ordinary balsamic vinegar, boil until thick and syrupy before adding to your favorite salad dressing. This will give it a more aged balsamic flavor.

Roquefort Salad Dressing

YIELD: 2 CUPS

1 cup nonfat yogurt
1/2 cup mayonnaise
1 shallot, minced
1 tablespoon lemon juice
1 teaspoon Worcestershire sauce
1/4 teaspoon freshly ground pepper,
    or to taste
3 ounces Roquefort or bleu cheese,
    crumbled

Combine the yogurt, mayonnaise, shallot, lemon juice, Worcestershire sauce and pepper in a bowl and mix well. Fold in the cheese.

Chill, covered, for several hours to allow the flavors to marry. Bring to room temperature before serving.

Soups
&
Sandwiches

Roasted Butternut Squash Bisque *page 54*

Melon Soup

1 honeydew melon, chopped
   (3 cups)
1/2 cup fresh orange juice
1/2 cup low-fat vanilla yogurt
1 tablespoon honey
1 teaspoon grated fresh ginger
2 teaspoons fresh lime juice
2 cups chopped peeled peaches
1 cup blueberries

Combine the melon, orange juice, yogurt,
honey, ginger and lime juice in a blender
and process until smooth. Stir in the
peaches and blueberries. Chill, covered,
until serving time. Ladle into soup bowls.

Summer Tomato Soup

12 ripe tomatoes, peeled and
   cut into quarters
6 green onions, trimmed and cut
   into 2-inch pieces
1 1/2 cups sour cream
3 tablespoons fresh lime juice
   (1 lime)
1 tablespoon curry powder
1 teaspoon salt
1 teaspoon sugar
1 teaspoon Worcestershire sauce
1/2 teaspoon whole marjoram
1/2 teaspoon thyme
8 to 10 drops of Tabasco sauce
freshly ground pepper to taste
chopped fresh chives

Combine the tomatoes, green onions,
sour cream, lime juice, curry powder, salt,
sugar and Worcestershire sauce in a food
processor or blender. Add the marjoram,
thyme, Tabasco sauce and pepper and
process until blended.

Chill, covered, in the refrigerator. Ladle into
soup bowls and garnish with chopped fresh
chives. You may substitute two 20-ounce
cans of tomatoes for the fresh tomatoes.

Fresh Asparagus Soup

YIELD: 4 SERVINGS

1 pound asparagus spears, trimmed
3/4 cup chopped onion
1/2 cup vegetable broth
1 tablespoon butter
2 tablespoons all-purpose flour
1 teaspoon salt
1/16 teaspoon freshly ground pepper
1 1/4 cups vegetable broth
1 cup soy milk or whole milk
1/2 cup yogurt
1 teaspoon lemon juice
1/4 cup (1 ounce) grated Parmesan
   cheese (optional)

Combine the asparagus, onion and 1/2 cup broth in a saucepan and bring to a boil. Reduce the heat and simmer until the vegetables are tender. Reserve 4 asparagus tips for the garnish. Process the remaining asparagus mixture in a blender until puréed.

Melt the butter in the same saucepan and stir in the flour, salt and pepper. Cook for 2 minutes, stirring constantly; do not allow the flour to brown. Stir in 1 1/4 cups broth and increase the heat to high.

Cook until the mixture comes to a boil, stirring constantly. Stir in the asparagus purée and soy milk. Whisk in the yogurt and lemon juice. Cook just until heated through, stirring occasionally. Ladle into soup bowls, top with the reserved asparagus tips and sprinkle with the cheese.

Black Bean Soup

YIELD: 4 SERVINGS

1/2 cup chopped onion
1 garlic clove, minced
2 teaspoons vegetable oil
1 1/2 cups water
1 (14-ounce) can beef broth
1 (15-ounce) can black beans,
   drained and rinsed
1 (14-ounce) can stewed tomatoes
1/2 cup rice
1/3 cup medium picante sauce
   or salsa
1 teaspoon ground cumin
1/4 teaspoon oregano
2 tablespoons chopped fresh
   cilantro (optional)

Sauté the onion and garlic in the oil in a Dutch oven until the onion is tender. Add the water, broth, beans, undrained tomatoes, rice, picante sauce, cumin and oregano and mix well. Bring to a boil and reduce the heat.

Simmer, covered, for 20 to 25 minutes or until the rice is tender, stirring occasionally. Ladle into soup bowls and sprinkle with the cilantro.

1 or 2 onions, chopped
1 cup chopped bell pepper
2 tablespoons vegetable oil
3 boneless skinless chicken breasts,
     cooked and chopped
2 (16-ounce) cans Great Northern beans
2 (16-ounce) cans chicken broth
1 (10-ounce) package frozen white corn
1 (4-ounce) can diced green chiles
1 cup fresh parsley, chopped
1 teaspoon white pepper
1 teaspoon ground cumin
1 teaspoon salt
coriander to taste
fried tortilla strips

Sauté the onion and bell pepper in the oil in a Dutch oven until tender. Add the chicken, undrained beans, broth, corn, green chiles, parsley, white pepper, cumin, salt and coriander and mix well.

Simmer over low heat for 1 hour or until the desired consistency, stirring occasionally. Ladle into chili bowls and garnish with fried tortilla strips. You may combine all of the ingredients except the tortilla chips in a slow cooker and cook for 6 hours or to the desired consistency, stirring occasionally.

Cream of Cauliflower Soup

YIELD: 6 TO 8 SERVINGS

1 large onion, chopped
2 shallots, chopped
1 tablespoon olive oil
2 (14-ounce) cans chicken broth
1 large head cauliflower, chopped
1 1/2 cups heavy cream
1 teaspoon salt
1/8 teaspoon white pepper

Sauté the onion and shallots in the olive oil in a Dutch oven until the onion is tender. Stir in the broth and bring to a boil. Add the cauliflower and cook for 15 minutes or until the cauliflower is tender, stirring occasionally. Process the cauliflower mixture in batches in a blender until puréed.

Return the purée to the Dutch oven and stir in the heavy cream, salt and white pepper. Cook over low heat until heated through, stirring frequently. Ladle into soup bowls and garnish with blanched fresh asparagus tips, cracked pepper or croutons.

Green Chile Cheese Soup

YIELD: 8 SERVINGS

3/4 cup finely chopped onion
1/2 cup minced celery
1/4 cup (1/2 stick) butter
2 tablespoons all-purpose flour
1 (16-ounce) can chicken broth
2 cups half-and-half
2 (4-ounce) cans diced green chiles
8 ounces Brie cheese, chopped
4 ounces bleu cheese, crumbled
1/2 teaspoon kosher salt
1/4 teaspoon freshly ground pepper
1/4 teaspoon thyme

Sauté the onion and celery in the butter in a large saucepan until the onion is tender. Add the flour and stir until combined. Stir in the broth and half-and-half in the order listed, mixing well after each addition. Add the green chiles and mix well.

Stir the Brie cheese, bleu cheese, salt, pepper and thyme into the soup mixture. Simmer until the cheese melts, stirring frequently. Ladle into soup bowls and serve immediately.

Potato Pancetta Chowder

YIELD: 4 SERVINGS

Serve Potato Pancetta Chowder with Rainbow Cheese Toasts (page 91), a wedge of Lettuce with Parmesan Dressing (page 45), and Cinnamon Flats with ice cream (page 203) for a relaxing meal at home.

4 ounces pancetta or
   thick-slice bacon
1 large or 2 medium leek
   bulbs, chopped
1 cup shiitake mushrooms or
   favorite mushrooms, chopped
1 tablespoon olive oil (optional)
$1/4$ cup all-purpose flour
1 cup half-and-half
$1/2$ teaspoon crushed dried thyme,
   or $1^1/2$ teaspoons minced
   fresh thyme
2 cups chicken broth
2 cups milk
1 pound fingerling or Yukon gold
   potatoes, cooked and sliced
$1/4$ teaspoon Tabasco sauce
salt and pepper to taste
chopped fresh chives or
   shredded cheese

Fry the pancetta in a Dutch oven for 3 minutes per side or until brown and crisp. Remove the pancetta to a paper towel to drain, reserving the pan drippings. Chop the pancetta. Sauté the leek and mushrooms in the reserved pan drippings for 5 minutes or until tender and light brown, adding the olive oil if needed. Add the flour and stir until the oil is absorbed. Stir in the half-and-half and thyme.

Cook over low heat until thickened, stirring constantly. Add the broth and milk and mix well. Stir in the pancetta, potatoes and Tabasco sauce. Season lightly with salt and generously with pepper. Simmer for 5 minutes, stirring occasionally. Ladle into soup bowls and sprinkle with chives and/or shredded cheese.

COMPLIMENTS OF

Roasted Red Pepper Soup

YIELD: 6 TO 8 SERVINGS

5 red bell peppers, cut into quarters
1/4 cup (1/2 stick) butter
1 tablespoon olive oil
3 carrots, finely chopped
3 shallots, finely chopped
1 pear, peeled and chopped
2 garlic cloves, minced
3 (16-ounce) cans chicken broth
1/2 to 1 teaspoon cayenne pepper

Arrange the bell pepper quarters in a single layer on a baking sheet and broil until blistered and charred on all sides, turning occasionally. Place the bell peppers in a nonrecycled paper bag and seal tightly. Peel, seed and chop the bell peppers when cool.

Heat the butter and olive oil in a 3-quart saucepan. Add the roasted bell peppers, carrots, shallots, pear and garlic to the butter mixture and sauté until tender. Reduce the heat to low and stir in the broth.

Simmer for 25 minutes, stirring occasionally. Stir in the cayenne pepper. Purée the soup mixture in batches in a blender or food processor. Return the purée to the saucepan and simmer just until heated through, stirring occasionally; do not allow to boil. Ladle the soup into clear glass or crystal wine glasses and garnish with sour cream and minced fresh chives.

Creamy Squash Soup

YIELD: 6 SERVINGS

4 or 5 squash, thinly sliced
2 onions, thinly sliced
1 large baking potato, thinly sliced
1 1/4 cups chicken broth
1 1/4 cups water
1 tablespoon parsley flakes
1/4 teaspoon ground cumin
    (optional)
salt and pepper to taste
1/4 cup (1/2 stick) butter
half-and-half to taste
sour cream (optional)

Combine the squash, onions, potato, broth, water, parsley flakes, cumin, salt and pepper in a large saucepan and mix well. Cook for 20 minutes or until the vegetables are tender, stirring occasionally.

Drain, reserving the vegetables and liquid. Process the vegetables in a blender or food processor until puréed. Add the butter and process until blended. Return the purée to the saucepan and add the reserved liquid and half-and-half until the desired consistency. Cook just until heated through or chill in the refrigerator. Ladle into soup bowls and top with a dollop of sour cream.

SOUPS & SANDWICHES

Roasted Butternut Squash Bisque

YIELD: 8 SERVINGS

Marmalade Cream

1 cup sour cream	1/2 teaspoon curry powder
2 tablespoons orange marmalade	1/4 teaspoon ground nutmeg

Squash Bisque

1 (3-pound) butternut squash	2 teaspoons curry powder
2 Granny Smith apples, peeled and cut into eighths	1 teaspoon salt
2 large onions, cut into 1-inch pieces	1/2 teaspoon freshly ground pepper
2 to 2 1/2 cups chicken broth	1 cup heavy cream
1 cup fresh orange juice	1/2 cup milk
2 teaspoons grated orange zest	chopped chives

For the cream, combine the sour cream, marmalade, curry powder and nutmeg in a bowl and mix well. Chill, covered, for 8 hours.

For the bisque, preheat the oven to 400 degrees. Line a baking sheet with foil and spray with nonstick cooking spray. Cut the squash into halves and remove the seeds. Arrange the squash halves cut side down on the prepared baking sheet. Surround with the apples and onions. Roast for 45 minutes or until tender. Let stand until cool.

Scoop the squash pulp into a Dutch oven, discarding the shells. Add the roasted apples, roasted onions, broth, orange juice, orange zest, curry powder, salt and pepper and mix well. Bring to a boil and reduce the heat to medium-low.

Simmer for 5 minutes, stirring frequently. Remove from the heat and let stand until cool. Process the squash mixture 1 cup at a time in a blender until puréed. You may prepare in advance up to this point and store, covered, in the refrigerator until just before serving. Return the purée to the Dutch oven and cook over low heat until heated through, stirring occasionally. Add the heavy cream and milk gradually, stirring constantly. Cook just until heated through, stirring occasionally. Ladle into soup bowls and top each serving with some of the Marmalade Cream in a decorative pattern. Garnish with chopped chives.

Photograph for this recipe on page 46.

COMPLIMENTS OF

YIELD: 8 SERVINGS

4 ounces prosciutto, chopped
2 eggs, lightly beaten
10 tablespoons coarsely grated
    Parmesan cheese
6 tablespoons fresh bread crumbs
1/4 cup Italian parsley, finely chopped
2 tablespoons Italian seasoning
freshly ground pepper to taste
1 pound ground veal
3 tablespoons olive oil
2 cups finely chopped onions
2 teaspoons minced garlic
8 cups shredded escarole
8 cups chicken stock
kosher salt to taste
grated Parmesan cheese

Mix the prosciutto, eggs, 10 tablespoons cheese, the bread crumbs, parsley, Italian seasoning and pepper in a bowl until combined. Add the veal to the prosciutto mixture and mix well. Shape the veal mixture into 1-inch balls.

Heat 1 tablespoon of the olive oil in a Dutch oven over medium-high heat until hot but not smoking. Add the meatballs to the hot oil and cook until brown on all sides; do not overcook. Remove to paper towels to drain, reserving the pan drippings.

Heat the remaining 2 tablespoons olive oil with the reserved pan drippings and add the onions. Cook until the onions are tender, stirring frequently. Stir in the garlic and cook for 2 minutes. Add the escarole and cook, covered, for 3 minutes or until wilted. Stir in the meatballs, stock, salt and pepper and bring to a boil.

Simmer for 15 minutes, stirring occasionally. Ladle into soup bowls and sprinkle with additional cheese. Serve with Italian bread and a mixed green salad.

TOMATO BASIL SOUP

Combine one 25-ounce jar tomato basil pasta sauce and 25 ounces of half-and-half in a saucepan and mix well. Cook just until heated through; do not allow to boil. Ladle into soup bowls and garnish with fresh basil.

1 tablespoon olive oil
5 garlic cloves, thinly sliced or
    chopped
3 (15-ounce) cans fat-free low-
    sodium chicken broth
$^1/_2$ cup dry white wine
2 (9-ounce) packages fresh three-
    cheese tortellini
$1^1/_4$ cups chopped fresh tomatoes,
    or 1 (16-ounce) can petite-cut
    tomatoes, drained
6 ounces baby spinach, trimmed
1 tablespoon butter
grated Parmesan cheese

Heat the olive oil in a Dutch oven over medium heat and add the garlic. Cook for 30 seconds, stirring constantly. Stir in the broth and wine and bring to a boil.

Cook for 2 minutes. Add the pasta and cook for 6 minutes, stirring occasionally. Stir in the tomatoes and spinach and cook for 2 minutes. Add the butter and cook just until the butter melts.

Ladle into soup bowls and sprinkle with Parmesan cheese. Serve immediately with crusty French bread or breadsticks. You may substitute meat-stuffed or mushroom-stuffed tortellini for the cheese tortellini.

Tuscan Sausage and Pepper Stew

YIELD: 6 TO 8 SERVINGS

1 pound link sausage
8 ounces cremini mushrooms,
    cut into halves
2 tablespoons olive oil
1 large onion, cut into eighths
1 yellow bell pepper, cut into strips
1 orange bell pepper, cut into strips
1 red bell pepper, cut into strips
3 garlic cloves, finely chopped
1 cup cut fresh green beans
1 (14-ounce) can diced tomatoes
$1/2$ cup red wine
1 teaspoon oregano
$1/4$ to $1/2$ teaspoon hot red pepper flakes
salt and black pepper to taste
2 tablespoons julienned fresh basil
grated Parmesan or Romano cheese

Preheat the oven to 375 degrees. Combine the sausage and $1/2$ of the mushrooms in a skillet and cook until the sausage is brown on all sides; drain. Heat the olive oil in a skillet and add the onion, bell peppers and garlic. Cook for 3 to 4 minutes, stirring frequently. Stir in the green beans and cook for 3 to 4 minutes. Add the undrained tomatoes, wine, oregano, hot red pepper flakes, salt and black pepper and mix well.

Cook for 3 to 4 minutes longer and spoon into a baking dish. Top with the remaining mushrooms, basil and sausage mixture. Bake for 40 minutes. Ladle into bowls and sprinkle with cheese. Serve with crusty bread and a mixed green salad.

YIELD: 8 SERVINGS

1 tablespoon vegetable oil
1 (3$^1/_2$- to 4-pound) chicken,
    cut up
$^2/_3$ cup vegetable oil
$^1/_2$ cup all-purpose flour
1$^1/_4$ pounds Creole, Polish or
    French smoked sausage, cut
    into $^1/_2$-inch slices
8 ounces lean baked ham, cut
    into $^1/_2$-inch pieces
2 cups chopped onions
$^1/_2$ cup chopped green
    bell pepper

$^1/_2$ cup thinly sliced shallot tops
2 tablespoons minced
    fresh parsley
3 garlic cloves, minced
8 cups cold water
3 bay leaves, crushed
1$^1/_4$ teaspoons thyme
1 teaspoon freshly ground
    black pepper
$^1/_8$ teaspoon cayenne pepper
2$^1/_2$ to 3 tablespoons filé powder
hot cooked rice

Preheat the oven to 175 degrees. Heat 1 tablespoon oil in a heavy 7- or 8-quart stockpot over high heat. Add the chicken to the hot oil and cook until brown on all sides. Remove the chicken to a baking dish using a slotted spoon and keep warm in the oven, discarding the pan drippings.

Heat $^2/_3$ cup oil in the stockpot over high heat until hot and gradually stir in the flour. Reduce the heat and cook until the roux is medium brown in color, stirring constantly. Add the sausage, ham, onions, bell pepper, shallot tops, parsley and garlic and mix well.

Cook for 10 minutes, stirring constantly. Add $^1/_4$ cup of the cold water, the chicken, bay leaves, thyme, black pepper and cayenne pepper and mix well. Add the remaining water gradually. Increase the heat and bring to a boil, stirring occasionally. Reduce the heat to low and simmer for 50 to 60 minutes or until the chicken is cooked through, being careful to retain the shape of the chicken pieces. Remove from the heat and let stand for 2 to 3 minutes. Stir in the filé powder and let stand for 5 minutes. Ladle over hot cooked rice in gumbo bowls.

Creole Bouillabaisse

YIELD: 8 SERVINGS

2 tablespoons butter or margarine	1 bay leaf
2 tablespoons olive oil	1/2 teaspoon salt
1/4 cup flour	1/4 teaspoon saffron threads, crushed
1 cup chopped onion	1/8 teaspoon cayenne pepper, or to taste
1/2 cup chopped celery	
1 garlic clove, minced	2 pounds fish fillets, cut into 6 to 8 portions
5 cups fish stock or water	
1 (28-ounce) can diced tomatoes	8 ounces peeled fresh shrimp
1/2 cup dry white wine	1 pint oysters
2 tablespoons chopped fresh parsley	6 ounces fresh crab meat, drained and shells removed
1 tablespoon fresh lemon juice	chopped fresh parsley

Heat the butter and olive oil in a stockpot over medium-high heat and gradually whisk in the flour. Cook until the roux is light brown in color, stirring constantly. Stir in the onion, celery and garlic and cook for 5 to 8 minutes or until the vegetables begin to brown. Add the stock gradually, stirring constantly. Add the undrained tomatoes, wine, parsley, lemon juice, bay leaf, salt, saffron and cayenne pepper and mix well. Stir in 1/4 of the fish.

Bring to a boil and reduce the heat to medium-low. Simmer for 20 minutes, stirring occasionally. Add the remaining fish and cook for 5 to 8 minutes. Stir in the shrimp, oysters and crab meat and cook for 5 to 10 minutes longer or until the shrimp turn pink. Discard the bay leaf and ladle the bouillabaisse into soup bowls. Garnish each serving with chopped fresh parsley.

SOUPS & SANDWICHES

New England Clam Chowder

PARMESAN CRISPS

Line a baking sheet with baking parchment or a silicone baking sheet. Mound 2 tablespoons finely shredded Parmesan cheese per crisp on the prepared baking sheet and flatten lightly with a fork; do not allow the sides to touch. Bake at 400 degrees until golden brown. Immediately remove to a wire rack to cool. Store in an airtight container. Serve with your favorite soups.

1 large onion, chopped
1 tablespoon bacon drippings
2 cups clam juice
2 cups chopped potatoes
2 cups milk
1 (8-ounce) container whipped
    cream cheese
2 cups clams, chopped
chopped fresh chives

Sauté the onion in the bacon drippings in a 6-quart Dutch oven until tender. Add the clam juice and potatoes and cook until the potatoes are tender, stirring occasionally. Stir in the milk, cream cheese and clams.

Cook for 10 minutes or until the cream cheese melts, stirring occasionally; do not allow to boil. Ladle into soup bowls and sprinkle with chopped chives. Serve with crusty French bread and a mixed green salad.

Soup is cuisine's kindest course.

—Kitchen Grafitti

COMPLIMENTS OF

Spinach and Oyster Chowder

YIELD: 6 TO 8 SERVINGS

2 potatoes
8 ounces fresh spinach,
 trimmed
1 onion, chopped
1/4 cup chopped celery
2 tablespoons vegetable oil
1/2 cup (1 stick) butter
2 tablespoons all-purpose flour
1 1/2 cups milk
1 cup heavy cream
1 cup (4 ounces) shredded
 sharp Cheddar cheese

1/2 cup (2 ounces) shredded
 Swiss cheese
2 tablespoons chopped
 fresh parsley
1 tablespoon Old Bay seasoning
1/4 teaspoon ground nutmeg
1/2 teaspoon pepper
1 quart oysters with liquor
1/8 teaspoon Tabasco sauce
chopped fresh parsley or chives

Combine the potatoes with enough water to cover in a saucepan and bring to a boil. Boil for 10 minutes or until tender; drain. Peel and chop the potatoes. Combine the spinach with a small amount of water in a saucepan and cook for 10 minutes. Drain and chop the spinach. Sauté the onion and celery in the oil in a skillet until the onion is tender; drain.

Melt the butter in a large saucepan and stir in the flour. Cook until paste consistency, stirring constantly. Reduce the heat and gradually stir in the milk and heavy cream. Cook until thickened, stirring constantly. Add the Cheddar cheese, Swiss cheese, parsley, Old Bay seasoning, nutmeg and pepper and mix well.

Cook until the cheese melts, stirring frequently; do not allow to boil. Add the potatoes, spinach and onion mixture and mix well. Stir in the undrained oysters and Tabasco sauce and simmer for 10 minutes. Ladle into soup bowls and sprinkle with parsley or chives. Serve with onion bread or tomato bread.

Cucumber Yummies

1 cup sour cream
1 envelope ranch salad dressing mix
sliced peeled cucumbers
tarragon vinegar
thinly sliced white bread, crusts
    trimmed and cut into shapes
basil chiffonade

Mix the sour cream and dressing mix in a bowl. Chill, covered, in the refrigerator. Combine sliced cucumbers with enough vinegar to cover in a shallow dish. Marinate at room temperature for 1 hour or longer; drain.

Cut the bread slices into the desired shapes. Spread the sour cream mixture on 1 side of each bread slice and top with cucumber slices and basil chiffonade. Serve open-faced or top with another bread slice.

Cucumber Salmon Sandwiches

8 ounces cream cheese, softened
1 small cucumber, peeled, seeded
    and chopped
2 teaspoons chopped fresh dill weed
1 teaspoon fresh lemon juice
$1/4$ teaspoon salt
$1/4$ teaspoon ground red pepper
12 miniature bagels, split
6 ounces smoked salmon,
    thinly sliced
24 cucumber slices
sprigs of dill weed

Combine the cream cheese, chopped cucumber, chopped dill weed, lemon juice, salt and red pepper in a food processor and process until combined. Chill, covered, for 1 hour.

Arrange the bagels cut side up on a baking sheet and broil until light brown. Spread the cream cheese mixture on the toasted side of each bagel and layer with smoked salmon. Garnish each sandwich with 1 cucumber slice and a sprig of dill weed.

Egg and Olive
Party Sandwiches

YIELD: 2 DOZEN SANDWICHES

6 hard-cooked eggs, finely chopped
1 (3-ounce) jar green olives, drained
    and finely chopped
4 ribs celery, finely chopped
1 cup pecans, finely chopped
2 cups mayonnaise
1/4 teaspoon Tabasco sauce
pepper to taste
2 small loaves sandwich bread,
    crusts trimmed

Combine the eggs, olives, celery and
pecans in a bowl and mix well. Stir in the
mayonnaise and Tabasco sauce and season
to taste with pepper. Chill, covered, for
8 to 10 hours.

Spread the egg mixture over 1/2 of the
bread slices and top with the remaining
bread slices. Cut each sandwich diagonally
into halves.

Gouda and Apple
Sandwiches

YIELD: 2 SANDWICHES

1/2 Golden Delicious apple or any
    variety apple, sliced
2 tablespoons unsalted butter
2 teaspoons Dijon mustard
4 slices white bread
2 teaspoons mango chutney
2 (1/4-inch) slices Gouda cheese

Sauté the apple in the butter in a skillet
for 4 to 6 minutes or until tender, turning
occasionally. Drain on a paper towel.

Spread the Dijon mustard on 2 slices
of bread and the chutney on the other
2 slices, then layer with the cheese. Top
with the sautéed apple and the remaining
bread slices, mustard side down. Grill
the sandwiches in a nonstick skillet until
the cheese melts and the bread is toasted.
Cut each sandwich diagonally into halves
and serve immediately.

FRIED GREEN TOMATO SANDWICHES

Fry 8 green tomato slices (page 12) and drain. Cook 12 slices bacon in a skillet until brown and crisp and drain. Spread White Rémoulade Sauce (page 131) on 1 side of 8 slices of toasted artisan bread. Layer 4 of the bread slices equally with the bacon and tomato slices and sprinkle each with 1 tablespoon julienned fresh basil. Top with the remaining bread slices sauce side down and cut diagonally into halves. This is a true Southern delight.

16 slices white bread, crusts
   trimmed
8 slices ham
8 slices turkey
8 slices medium Cheddar cheese
6 eggs
3 cups milk
$^{1}/_{2}$ teaspoon onion salt
$^{1}/_{2}$ teaspoon dry mustard
$^{1}/_{8}$ teaspoon Worcestershire sauce
2 cups crushed cornflakes
$^{1}/_{2}$ cup (1 stick) butter, melted

Line the bottoms of a greased 9×13 baking dish and a greased 7×11-inch baking dish with $^{1}/_{2}$ of the bread slices. Layer each bread slice with 1 slice of ham, 1 slice of turkey and 1 slice of cheese. Top with the remaining bread slices to form 8 sandwiches.

Whisk the eggs in a bowl until blended. Stir in the milk, onion salt, dry mustard and Worcestershire sauce and pour the egg mixture over the sandwiches. Chill, covered, for 8 to 10 hours.

Preheat the oven to 350 degrees. Toss the cornflakes and butter in a bowl until coated and sprinkle the crumb mixture over the top of the chilled layers. Bake for 1 to 1$^{1}/_{4}$ hours or until set. Serve with a mixed green salad for a luncheon or for brunch with sliced fruit.

COMPLIMENTS OF

Grilled Vegetable Panini

YIELD: 4 SERVINGS

8 slices ciabatta or crusty sandwich rolls
butter or olive oil
roasted or grilled sliced eggplant, onion and/or squash
1 (12-ounce) jar roasted red peppers, drained
4 to 8 slices smoked Gouda cheese
1/4 cup julienned fresh basil

Brush 1 side of each bread slice with butter or olive oil. Layer 1/2 of the bread slices with roasted eggplant, roasted onion and/or roasted squash, roasted red peppers, cheese and basil. Top with the remaining bread slices butter side up. Grill on a panini press or in a skillet until brown and crisp on both sides.

Or, try these combinations: roasted tomatoes, fresh mozzarella cheese, fresh basil leaves, kosher salt and freshly ground pepper; prosciutto, roasted eggplant, mozzarella cheese, salt and pepper; roasted bell peppers, provolone cheese, salt and pepper.

Arrange platters of roasted vegetables, cheese, condiments, fresh herbs and/or olives on a serving table and allow your guests to create their own sandwiches. Use your imagination, as the combinations are endless.

Too few people understand a really good sandwich.

—*James Beard*

Layer some of these combinations on any flavor tortilla at your next party or tailgate gathering: roast beef, provolone cheese, arugula, thinly sliced tomatoes, and mayonnaise; thinly sliced roasted chicken, guacamole, Monterey Jack cheese, and shredded lettuce; sliced ham, herb-seasoned cheese spread, fresh basil, and thinly sliced red onion; Swiss cheese, sliced mushrooms, sliced avocado, fresh spinach, sun-dried tomatoes, and honey mustard dressing. Be creative!

1 (2-ounce) tub herb-seasoned
  cheese spread
mayonnaise
4 (12-inch) sun-dried tomato,
  spinach, wheat or
  flour tortillas
1 pound roasted turkey breast,
  sliced
2 bunches green onions, chopped
10 ounces baby spinach leaves,
  stemmed
8 ounces bacon, crisp-cooked and
  crumbled

Combine the herbed cheese spread with enough mayonnaise in a bowl until a spreading consistency. Spread the cheese mixture over 1 side of each tortilla. Layer the tortillas evenly with the turkey, green onions, spinach and bacon. Roll tightly and wrap each roll individually in plastic wrap. Chill for several hours.

Cut each roll diagonally into halves and stand on ends on serving plates, or cut each roll into 1/2-inch slices and secure with wooden picks. Substitute ham or roast beef for the turkey and fresh basil for the spinach if desired.

COMPLIMENTS OF

Vegetable

Tea Sandwiches

YIELD: 40 TO 50 SMALL SANDWICHES

2 tomatoes, peeled and minced
1 cucumber, minced
1 green bell pepper, minced
3/4 cup minced celery
1 small onion, minced
2 carrots, minced
juice of 1/2 lemon
1 envelope unflavored gelatin
1 teaspoon salt
1/4 cup hot water
2 cups mayonnaise
thinly sliced white or wheat bread,
    crusts trimmed

Drain the tomatoes, cucumber, bell pepper, celery, onion and carrots in a colander. Combine the lemon juice with enough cold water in a bowl to measure 1/4 cup. Soften the gelatin in the lemon juice mixture and stir in the salt. Add the hot water and stir until the gelatin dissolves.

Press the vegetables lightly to remove any remaining moisture and spoon into a bowl. Stir in the gelatin mixture and mayonnaise. Chill, covered, for 8 to 10 hours or for several days. Spread on bread slices.

You may prepare sandwiches up to 1 day in advance and store, covered with damp paper towels and plastic wrap, in the refrigerator. Cut the sandwiches into triangles, strips or rounds. Or, spoon the spread into a crock and serve with crackers.

Gourmet

Pimento Cheese

YIELD: 3 CUPS

1 1/2 cups (6 ounces) grated
    Parmesan cheese
1 cup (4 ounces) shredded
    Cheddar cheese
1 cup (4 ounces) shredded smoked
    Gouda cheese
1 (7-ounce) jar diced pimentos,
    drained
1 cup mayonnaise
1 jalapeño, seeded and minced
1 tablespoon vinegar
1 teaspoon salt
1 teaspoon black pepper
cayenne pepper to taste

Combine the Parmesan cheese, Cheddar cheese, Gouda cheese and pimentos in a bowl and mix well. Mix the mayonnaise, jalapeño, vinegar, salt, black pepper and cayenne pepper in a bowl and stir into the cheese mixture. Chill, covered, in the refrigerator.

Use as a sandwich filling or a spread for crackers or as a dip. Substitute Colby cheese or Monterey Jack cheese for 1 of the cheeses listed above if desired.

67

Brunch
&
Breads

The Bridgewater House French Toast *page 81*

Baked Eggs with Smoked Salmon

YIELD: 4 SERVINGS

POACHED EGGS

Crack eggs into simmering

water in a saucepan and add

2 tablespoons of vinegar.

Cook the eggs until the white

is firm. Remove the eggs with

a slotted spoon to a bowl of

ice water. To reheat, place the

poached eggs in simmering

water for 2 to 3 minutes.

3 tablespoons unsalted butter
1 small leek, cut into halves and
    thinly sliced
6 ounces smoked salmon,
    finely flaked
$1/2$ cup heavy cream
salt and pepper to taste
4 eggs
8 teaspoons snipped fresh chives

Heat the butter in a saucepan and add the leek. Cook, covered, for 8 minutes or until tender. Remove from the heat and stir in the salmon and $1/3$ of the heavy cream. Season to taste with salt and pepper. Spoon the salmon mixture into 4 buttered ramekins and let stand until cool.

Preheat the oven to 325 degrees. Make an indentation in the center of the salmon mixture with the back of a teaspoon and fill each indentation with 1 egg. Pour equal portions of the remaining heavy cream over each egg and sprinkle with salt, pepper and 2 teaspoons of the snipped chives.

Arrange the ramekins in a baking pan and add enough boiling water to the baking pan to come halfway up the sides of the ramekins. Bake for 20 to 25 minutes or until set. The yolks should tremble when lightly shaken. Garnish with additional snipped chives and serve immediately with buttered toast.

COMPLIMENTS OF

Creole Eggs

Creole Sauce
1 bell pepper, chopped
1 rib celery, chopped
1 onion, chopped
2 tablespoons butter
1 (28-ounce) can tomatoes,
    chopped
1 tablespoon sugar
salt and pepper to taste

White Sauce and Assembly
2 tablespoons butter
2 tablespoons all-purpose flour
1 cup milk
4 eggs, hard-cooked and sliced
cracker crumbs

For the Creole sauce, sauté the bell
pepper, celery and onion in the butter
in a saucepan until the onion is tender.
Stir in the undrained tomatoes and sugar
and cook over low heat until thickened.
Season to taste with salt and pepper.

For the white sauce, preheat the oven
to 350 degrees. Heat the butter in a
saucepan and stir in the flour. Cook until
blended and bubbly, stirring constantly.
Add the milk gradually and cook over low
heat until thickened, stirring constantly.

Layer the eggs, white sauce, Creole sauce
and cracker crumbs in a baking dish.
Bake for 20 to 30 minutes or until heated
through. Serve with ham and/or grits.

Fresh Spring Frittata

*Serve with Cinni-Minis (page 87)
and Fruit Mélange (page 185) for a
simple weekend brunch.*

YIELD: 6 TO 8 SERVINGS

12 eggs
1/2 cup sour cream
1 teaspoon salt
1/4 teaspoon freshly ground pepper
1/4 teaspoon baking powder
1/8 teaspoon Tabasco sauce
1 (10-ounce) package frozen chopped
    spinach, thawed and drained
2 tablespoons butter
1/2 cup crumbled crisp-cooked bacon
5 large plum tomatoes, seeded
    and chopped
8 ounces Monterey Jack cheese,
    shredded
1/4 cup julienned fresh basil
sprigs of basil or parsley

Preheat the oven to 350 degrees. Combine
the eggs, sour cream, salt, pepper, baking
powder and Tabasco sauce in a mixing bowl
and beat at medium speed for 2 to 3 minutes
or until blended. Stir in the spinach.

Heat the butter in a 12-inch ovenproof skillet
and add the egg mixture, tilting the skillet to
ensure even coverage. Bake for 15 minutes.
Remove from the oven and sprinkle with the
bacon, tomatoes, cheese and julienned basil.
Bake for 15 to 20 minutes longer or until
set. Cut into wedges and garnish with
sprigs of basil.

BRUNCH & BREADS

Eggnog French Toast with Cranberry Maple Syrup

YIELD: 6 SERVINGS

To test raw eggs for freshness, place the eggs in a bowl of cold water. If fresh, the eggs will lie on their sides. If old, the eggs will stand upright.

French Toast
1 long loaf sourdough bread
1 quart eggnog
6 eggs
$^1/_2$ cup Southern Comfort
$^1/_2$ teaspoon ground nutmeg
$^1/_2$ teaspoon ground cinnamon
$^1/_2$ teaspoon ground allspice
clarified butter

Cranberry Maple Syrup
1 (16-ounce) bottle maple syrup
2 cups fresh cranberries
1 cinnamon stick

For the French toast, cut the bread loaf into $1^1/_2$-inch slices. Arrange the bread slices in a single layer in a baking pan or on a baking sheet with sides.

Whisk the eggnog, eggs, Southern Comfort, nutmeg, cinnamon and allspice in a bowl until combined and pour over the bread slices. Chill, covered, in the refrigerator for 8 to 10 hours.

Preheat the oven to 350 degrees. Fry the bread slices in clarified butter in a skillet until brown on both sides. Arrange the browned bread slices in a baking pan and bake until puffy.

For the syrup, combine the maple syrup, cranberries and cinnamon stick in a saucepan and mix well. Simmer for 45 minutes, stirring occasionally. Discard the cinnamon stick and serve the syrup warm with the French toast.

COMPLIMENTS OF

Bananas Foster Waffles

Brown Sugar Butter
$1/2$ cup (1 stick) unsalted butter, browned
$1/2$ cup plus 3 tablespoons packed brown sugar
1 to 2 teaspoons heavy cream

Waffles
$1^1/2$ cups all-purpose flour
$1/4$ cup granulated sugar
$1^1/2$ teaspoons baking soda
1 teaspoon salt
$1^1/2$ cups buttermilk
6 tablespoons butter, melted
2 eggs, beaten
4 bananas, sliced
$1/8$ teaspoon ground cinnamon
1 tablespoon banana liqueur
1 ounce brandy
confectioners' sugar to taste

For the brown sugar butter, mix the browned butter, brown sugar and heavy cream in a bowl.

For the waffles, preheat the oven to 200 degrees. Sift the flour, granulated sugar, baking soda and salt into a bowl and mix well. Whisk in the buttermilk, butter and eggs.

Preheat a waffle iron coated with nonstick cooking spray. Pour 1 cup of the batter per waffle onto the hot waffle iron and bake until brown using the manufacturer's directions. Arrange the waffles on a baking sheet and keep warm in the oven.

Combine 3 tablespoons of the Brown Sugar Butter, the bananas and cinnamon in a skillet and cook for 2 to 3 minutes, stirring frequently. Remove from the heat. Stir in the liqueur and brandy and ignite with a long match. Allow the flames to subside. Spoon the banana mixture evenly over the waffles on serving plates and sprinkle with confectioners' sugar. Serve immediately with crisp-cooked bacon, Canadian bacon or browned sausage links.

Cheesy Chive Muffins

YIELD: 2 DOZEN MUFFINS

HUSH PUPPIES

Combine 3 cups self-rising cornmeal, 1 cup all-purpose flour, 1 teaspoon pepper and 1 teaspoon salt in a bowl and mix well. Stir in 1 cup chopped onion. Add 2 cups buttermilk and 2 beaten eggs and mix until combined. Let stand for 15 minutes. Drop the batter by teaspoonfuls into 340-degree vegetable oil in a deep skillet and fry until golden brown; drain. Serve immediately.

$1/2$ cup chopped onion
1 tablespoon butter
$1^1/2$ cups baking mix
1 cup (4 ounces) shredded sharp
    Cheddar cheese
$1/4$ teaspoon salt
pepper to taste
1 egg, lightly beaten
$1/2$ cup milk
1 cup ground cooked ham
$1/4$ cup chopped fresh chives

Preheat the oven to 375 degrees. Cook the onion in the butter in a small skillet until tender, stirring frequently. Combine the onion mixture, baking mix, $1/2$ cup of the cheese, the salt and pepper in a bowl and mix well. Add the egg and milk and stir just until moistened.

Spray 24 to 30 miniature muffin cups with nonstick cooking spray or lightly grease. Spoon about $1^1/2$ teaspoons of the batter into each muffin cup. Top each with about 1 teaspoon of the ham, a pinch of the chives, 1 teaspoon of the remaining cheese and another pinch of the chives. The muffin cups should be $2/3$ full.

Bake for 12 minutes or until golden brown. Remove to a wire rack immediately. You may freeze for future use. Reheat in a 200-degree oven for 15 to 20 minutes.

COMPLIMENTS OF

Lemon Tea Bread

Lemon Bread

1 1/2 cups all-purpose flour
1 teaspoon baking powder
1/2 teaspoon salt
1/2 cup (1 stick) butter, softened
1 cup sugar
2 eggs
1/2 cup milk
1 tablespoon grated lemon zest

Lemon Glaze

1 cup confectioners' sugar
2 tablespoons fresh lemon juice
1 tablespoon grated lemon zest
1 tablespoon granulated sugar

For the bread, preheat the oven to 350 degrees. Mix the flour, baking powder and salt together. Beat the butter in a mixing bowl until creamy. Add the sugar gradually, beating constantly until light and fluffy. Add the eggs 1 at a time, beating well after each addition. Add the flour mixture alternately with the milk and beat at low speed just until blended, beginning and ending with the flour mixture. Stir in the lemon zest.

Spoon the batter into a greased and floured 4×8-inch loaf pan or 2 miniature loaf pans. Bake for 1 hour or until a wooden pick inserted in the center comes out clean. Cool in the pan for 10 minutes and remove to a wire rack.

For the glaze, mix the confectioners' sugar and lemon juice in a bowl until of a glaze consistency and drizzle over the warm loaf, allowing the excess to drip down the sides. Mix the lemon zest and granulated sugar in a bowl and sprinkle over the top of the loaf. Let stand until cool.

Brunch & Breads

Lemon Drop Cakes

1 (2-layer) package yellow
   cake mix
1¹/₂ pounds confectioners' sugar
grated zest and strained juice of
   2 large lemons
grated zest and strained juice of
   2 large oranges

Preheat the oven to 375 degrees. Prepare the cake mix using the package directions, omitting 3 tablespoons water. Drop the batter by teaspoonfuls into greased and floured miniature muffin cups. Bake for 10 to 12 minutes.

Combine the confectioners' sugar, lemon zest, lemon juice, orange zest and orange juice in a mixing bowl and beat until glaze consistency. Dip the hot cakes in the citrus glaze until coated on all sides. Remove the cakes with a slotted spoon to a sheet of waxed paper and let stand until set.

*Food is our common ground,
a universal experience.*

—James Beard

CROSTINI

Cut 1 baguette into sixteen ¹/₃-inch slices and toast at 400 degrees for 5 minutes per side. Rub the slices with a garlic clove and brush with ¹/₃ cup olive oil. Sprinkle with 1 teaspoon dried thyme, 1 teaspoon freshly ground pepper and 1 teaspoon kosher salt. Serve with soups and salads, or spread with your favorite savory topping. Store in a paper bag.

YIELD: 4 DOZEN CINNI-MINIS

Cinni-Minis

2 (8-count) cans crescent rolls
6 tablespoons butter, softened
$1/3$ cup packed brown sugar
1 tablespoon ground cinnamon
$1/4$ cup chopped pecans

Confectioners' Sugar Icing

$2/3$ cup confectioners' sugar
1 tablespoon milk
1 teaspoon vanilla extract
$1/8$ teaspoon salt

For the cinni-minis, preheat the oven to 375 degrees. Unroll the dough and separate each can into 4 rectangles. Mix the butter, brown sugar and cinnamon in a bowl until blended and spread the brown sugar mixture evenly on 1 side of each rectangle. Sprinkle with the pecans and, starting at the long end, roll each rectangle into a log. Cut each log into six 1-inch slices using a serrated knife. To make slicing easier, freeze the logs on a baking sheet for 10 minutes before slicing.

Arrange the slices cut side up $1/4$ inch apart in 2 greased 8-inch round pans and bake for 12 to 15 minutes or until golden brown. You may prepare 1 day in advance, store in the refrigerator and bake just before serving.

For the icing, combine the confectioners' sugar, milk, vanilla and salt in a bowl and mix until glaze consistency. Drizzle the icing over the warm rolls and serve immediately.

Homemade Biscuits

YIELD: 10 TO 12 BISCUITS

2 cups all-purpose flour
2 teaspoons baking powder
$1/2$ teaspoon salt
$1/4$ teaspoon baking soda
$1/4$ cup shortening
$2/3$ cup buttermilk

Preheat the oven to 450 degrees. Sift
the flour, baking powder, salt and baking
soda into a bowl and mix well. Cut in
the shortening until crumbly. Add the
buttermilk and mix just until moistened.

Roll or pat the dough $1/2$ inch thick
on a lightly floured surface. Cut with
a biscuit cutter and arrange the rounds
on an ungreased baking sheet. Bake for
12 to 15 minutes or until light brown.
Serve immediately.

Currant Scones

YIELD: 18 TO 24 SCONES

$3^1/2$ cups self-rising flour
1 cup (scant) sugar
6 tablespoons butter, chilled
$3/4$ cup buttermilk
1 cup dried currants or raisins
grated zest of 1 large orange

Preheat the oven to 400 degrees. Combine
the self-rising flour, sugar and butter in a
food processor and process until crumbly.
Add the buttermilk, currants and orange
zest and process just until a dough forms;
do not overmix.

Pat the dough $1/2$ to $3/4$ inch thick on a
lightly floured surface and cut into rounds.
Arrange the rounds on a greased baking
sheet and bake for 18 to 20 minutes or
until light brown. Serve with jam and/or
clotted cream.

Food is not only essential to sustain life;
it is also an exquisite pleasure.

COMPLIMENTS OF

YIELD: 3 DOZEN ROLLS

2 envelopes dry yeast
$1/3$ cup warm (110 degrees) water
1 cup shortening, melted and cooled to 110 degrees
$2/3$ cup sugar
4 eggs, beaten
2 teaspoons salt
$1^1/3$ cups warm (110 degrees) water
5 cups all-purpose flour
melted butter

Dissolve the yeast in $1/3$ cup warm water in a bowl. Combine the shortening and sugar in a bowl and mix well. Stir in the yeast mixture, eggs and salt. Mix in $1^1/3$ cups warm water. Add the flour and stir until a soft dough forms.

Shape the dough into a ball and place in a greased bowl, turning to coat the surface. Let rise, covered loosely, for 2 hours or until doubled in bulk. Punch down the dough and roll $3/4$ inch thick on a lightly floured surface. Cut into desired size.

Arrange 1 inch apart on a greased baking sheet. Brush the tops with melted butter and let rise until doubled in bulk. Preheat the oven to 325 degrees and bake for 25 minutes.

News Of Bygone Days
(From The Commercial Appeal Files)

75 YEARS AGO
May 4, 1886

Members of the Women's Exchange have arranged to serve hot suppers to those who wish to avoid having to go home after the races at Montgomery Park. After the day's sport the sportsmen and their ladies may get off the street cars at the head of Vance and be near the site where the Exchange is serving the hot meals.

YIELD: 16 TO 20 SERVINGS

GARLIC BREAD

Heat 1/4 cup butter in a saucepan until melted and stir in 1/4 cup chopped fresh parsley, 1 1/2 tablespoons olive oil and 2 to 3 tablespoons minced garlic. Split 1 baguette lengthwise into halves and brush the garlic mixture over the cut sides of the baguette. Wrap in foil and bake at 325 degrees for 20 minutes.

1 loaf Italian bread
olive oil
finely chopped garlic
4 ounces bleu cheese, crumbled
1/2 red onion, cut into
    paper-thin slices
freshly ground pepper to taste
16 to 20 kalamata olives, pitted
    and cut into halves
1 teaspoon finely chopped
    fresh rosemary
sprigs of rosemary

Preheat the oven to 400 degrees. Cut the loaf horizontally into halves. Cut a thin slice from the top half to form a flat base. Arrange the halves cut side up on a baking sheet lined with foil.

Brush the cut sides of the bread halves with olive oil and sprinkle with garlic and the cheese. Layer evenly with the onion slices, pepper and olives and sprinkle with chopped rosemary. Bake for 8 to 10 minutes or until the cheese melts. Cool for 2 minutes and cut into 1 1/2-inch slices.

Arrange the slices on a serving platter and garnish with sprigs of fresh rosemary. Serve warm. You may prepare up to 2 hours in advance and store, wrapped in plastic wrap, in the refrigerator. Bake as directed above just before serving.

COMPLIMENTS OF

— Rainbow Cheese Toasts —

YIELD: 2 DOZEN TOASTS

3 hoagie rolls, cut lengthwise
　　into eighths
1/2 cup (1 stick) butter, melted
4 ounces sharp Cheddar cheese,
　　shredded
4 ounces Monterey Jack cheese,
　　shredded
1 tablespoon garlic powder
1/2 teaspoon dill weed
1/2 cup (2 ounces) grated Parmesan
　　cheese or Romano cheese

Preheat the oven to 350 degrees. Dip the
hoagie slices in the butter and arrange in
a single layer in a 9×13-inch baking pan.
Sprinkle with the Cheddar cheese, Monterey
Jack cheese, garlic powder and dill weed.
Top with the Parmesan cheese.

Bake for 20 to 25 minutes or until the
cheese is light brown and bubbly. Serve with
soups, salads or stews. You may substitute
Dubliner Irish cheese and asiago cheese for
the Cheddar Cheese and Monterey Jack
cheese for a different twist.

— Stuffed Bread —

YIELD: 3 DOZEN SLICES

2 loaves French bread
2 cups (8 ounces) shredded
　　Cheddar cheese
1 cup (2 sticks) butter, softened
1 cup mayonnaise
1 bunch green onions, chopped
Crazy Jane salt to taste

Preheat the oven to 350 degrees. Cut each
bread loaf partially through into 3/4- to
1-inch-thick slices. Combine the cheese,
butter, mayonnaise, green onions and salt
in a bowl and mix well.

Spread the cheese mixture between the slices
and wrap each loaf in foil. Bake for 15 to
20 minutes or until heated through. Serve
immediately. You may prepare in advance
and store in the refrigerator. Bring to room
temperature and bake as directed above.

BRUNCH & BREADS

Meat & Game

Crown Roast of Lamb with
Winter Mint Wild Rice *page 100*

Forgotten Beef Tenderloin

YIELD: VARIABLE SERVINGS

1 (any size) beef tenderloin
seasonings to taste

Preheat the oven to 500 degrees for
30 minutes. Do not open the door. Season
the tenderloin with your favorite seasonings
and place in a baking pan. Bake for
5 minutes and turn off the oven.

Let the tenderloin stand in the oven with
the door closed for 1 hour; do not peek.
The tenderloin will be rare. If baking a rib
roast, bake for 5 minutes per pound and
allow the roast to stand in the oven for
2 hours. Reheat leftover tenderloin on the
grill for a smoky flavor.

Bleu Cheese Fillets

YIELD: 4 SERVINGS

4 ounces bleu cheese, crumbled
1 tablespoon butter, softened
1/4 cup A.1. steak sauce
1/4 cup Worcestershire sauce
1/8 teaspoon Tabasco sauce
4 beef fillets

Preheat the grill. Combine the cheese,
butter, steak sauce, Worcestershire sauce
and Tabasco sauce in a bowl and mix well.

Grill the fillets over hot coals to the desired
degree of doneness. Remove to a platter
and immediately spread a thin layer of the
cheese mixture over the top of each fillet.

COMPLIMENTS OF

Marinated Flank Steak

1 flank steak
$^1/_2$ cup olive oil
1 large garlic clove, crushed
2 tablespoons crumbled Roquefort cheese
2 tablespoons dry vermouth
2 teaspoons instant coffee granules
1 teaspoon kosher salt
$^1/_2$ teaspoon freshly ground pepper
$^1/_2$ teaspoon Dijon mustard

Score the flank steak. Combine the olive oil, garlic, cheese, vermouth, coffee granules, salt, pepper and Dijon mustard in a bowl and mix well. Pour the olive oil mixture over the steak in a shallow dish, turning and rubbing to coat. Marinate at room temperature for 1 hour.

Preheat the broiler or grill. Drain the steak, reserving the marinade. Broil or grill the steak for 5 minutes per side or to the desired degree of doneness. Bring the reserved marinade to a boil in a saucepan and boil for 5 minutes. Add the steak to the hot marinade and turn to coat. Cut the steak diagonally into slices and serve with the remaining warm marinade.

MEAT & GAME

Picadillo Empanadas

YIELD: 6 TO 8 SERVINGS

When making meat loaf, line the bottom of the baking pan or loaf pan with bread slices. The bread will absorb most of the fat released from the meat loaf as it bakes. Discard the bread before serving.

2 pounds ground round
1 1/2 cups finely chopped onions
1 1/2 cups finely chopped green
    bell peppers
8 garlic cloves, finely chopped
1 1/2 cups chopped golden raisins
1 cup drained diced pimentos
    (about two 7-ounce jars)
1/2 cup chopped drained capers
    (about 2 (3-ounce) jars)
1/2 cup tomato paste
4 teaspoons habanero sauce
1 teaspoon salt
flour tortillas

Preheat the oven to 350 degrees. Brown the ground round in a 10- to 12-inch skillet, stirring until crumbly; drain. Add the onions, bell peppers and garlic to the ground round and sauté for 5 minutes or until the onion is tender. Stir in the raisins, pimentos, capers, tomato paste, habanero sauce and salt and cook until heated through.

Reserve some of the ground round mixture for the topping. Spoon the remaining ground round mixture onto tortillas and roll tightly to enclose the filling. Arrange seam side down in a baking dish and sprinkle with the reserved ground round mixture.

Bake, covered with foil, for 15 to 20 minutes or until heated through. Serve with a mixed green salad tossed with mandarin oranges and a citrus vinaigrette. You may prepare in advance, store in the refrigerator and bake just before serving. Or, store in the freezer for up to 3 months.

Cinnamon Beef

YIELD: 4 SERVINGS

1/4 cup (1/2 stick) butter or
    margarine
1 pound beef round, cut into strips
1 onion, sliced
2 garlic cloves, minced
1 cup water
2 tablespoons soy sauce
1 teaspoon ground cinnamon
salt and pepper to taste
hot cooked rice
toasted coconut
sliced almonds

Heat the butter in a cast-iron skillet and add the beef. Cook until brown and remove to a platter using a slotted spoon, reserving the pan drippings. Add the onion and garlic to the reserved pan drippings and sauté until the onion is brown. Add the beef, water, soy sauce, cinnamon, salt and pepper to the onion mixture and mix well.

Simmer for 30 minutes or until the beef is tender, stirring occasionally. Spoon the beef mixture over hot cooked rice on a serving platter. Garnish with toasted coconut and sliced almonds.

Beef Bourguignon

YIELD: 8 TO 10 SERVINGS

8 slices bacon, finely chopped
4 pounds lean beef sirloin, trimmed
2 pounds fresh mushrooms, sliced
2 garlic cloves, crushed
2 bay leaves, crushed
2 tablespoons chopped fresh parsley
1 teaspoon each salt and thyme
1/8 teaspoon pepper
1/2 cup (1 stick) butter
1/2 cup all-purpose flour
1 1/2 (10-ounce) cans beef consommé
hot cooked rice

Cook the bacon in a Dutch oven until brown and crisp. Remove the bacon to a bowl using a slotted spoon, reserving the bacon drippings. Slice the beef with the grain into 1/2×4-inch strips and add the beef in batches to the reserved bacon drippings. Cook until brown, stirring frequently. Add the bacon, mushrooms, garlic, bay leaves, parsley, salt, thyme and pepper and mix well. Remove from the heat.

Heat the butter in a saucepan and stir in the flour. Cook until light brown in color, stirring constantly. Stir in the consommé and cook until slightly thickened. Add to the beef mixture and mix well.

Simmer, covered, for 1 1/2 hours or until the beef is tender. Adjust the seasonings and spoon over hot cooked rice.

A Moroccan lamb recipe garnished with Kalamata Tapenade (page 18) and served with Watercress and Pear Salad (page 32), Mushroom Onion Gratin (page 165), and Amaretto Freeze (page 184) will tempt the palate.

Cumin-Crusted Lamb Chops

YIELD: 4 SERVINGS

2 racks of lamb, cut into chops,
    or 8 loin chops
2 to 3 tablespoons extra-virgin
    olive oil
ground cumin to taste
Kalamata Tapenade (page 18)

Preheat the grill. Brush the lamb lightly with the olive oil and coat both sides with cumin. Grill over hot coals to the desired degree of doneness. Serve with Kalamata Tapenade.

*One cannot think well, love well, sleep well,
if one has not dined well.*

—Virginia Woolf

COMPLIMENTS OF

Broiled Marinated Lamb Chops

YIELD: 4 SERVINGS

8 lamb chops, 1 1/2 inches thick
salt and pepper to taste
3 garlic cloves, minced
4 teaspoons Dijon mustard
4 teaspoons soy sauce
4 teaspoons olive oil or butter
1 tablespoon chopped fresh rosemary, or
    1 teaspoon dried rosemary
sprigs of rosemary

Season the lamb with salt and pepper. Combine the garlic, Dijon mustard, soy sauce, olive oil and chopped rosemary in a shallow dish and mix well. Add the lamb to the garlic mixture and turn to coat. Marinate, covered, in the refrigerator for 1 hour, turning occasionally.

Preheat the broiler. Arrange the lamb on a broiler rack in a broiler pan and broil for 3 to 5 minutes per side or to the desired degree of doneness. Garnish with sprigs of fresh rosemary and serve with roasted asparagus and garlic mashed potatoes.

MEAT & GAME

Butterflied Leg of Lamb

YIELD: 8 TO 10 SERVINGS

1/2 cup fresh lemon juice
      (2 large lemons)
2 large garlic cloves, slivered
2 tablespoons olive oil
1 tablespoon Dijon mustard
1/8 teaspoon ground ginger
Salt and freshly ground pepper
      to taste
1 (6-pound) leg of lamb, butterflied
sprigs of rosemary
mint jelly

Combine the lemon juice, garlic, olive oil, Dijon mustard, ginger, salt and pepper in a bowl and mix well. Pour the lemon juice mixture over the lamb in a 2-gallon sealable plastic bag and seal tightly. Turn to coat. Marinate in the refrigerator for 2 to 3 hours.

Preheat the grill. Grill for 12 to 15 minutes per side or to the desired degree of doneness. Slice the lamb as desired and garnish with sprigs of rosemary. Serve with mint jelly.

Crown Roast of Lamb with Winter Mint Wild Rice

YIELD: 8 SERVINGS

1 crown roast of lamb
      (2 to 8 chop racks tied together)
2 teaspoons thyme
coarse salt and freshly ground
      pepper to taste
Winter Mint Wild Rice (page 155)
kumquats
sprigs of mint and watercress
mint jelly

Preheat the oven to 450 degrees. Season the lamb with thyme, salt and pepper and cover the bone tips with foil. Arrange the lamb in a shallow baking pan.

Roast for 30 minutes for medium-rare or 35 minutes for well-done. Remove to a serving platter and fill the center with the rice. Let stand for 10 minutes and carve as desired. Garnish with kumquats and sprigs of mint and watercress. Serve with mint jelly. You may prepare in advance and store in the refrigerator. Reheat before serving.

Photograph for this recipe on page 92.

COMPLIMENTS OF

Roasted Pork Tenderloin

Herbed Rice (page 154) and Haricot Vert Sauté (page 161) are good accompaniments to this dish. End with Fruit Sherbet (page 191).

YIELD: 6 SERVINGS

1 cup orange juice
1/3 cup soy sauce
1/4 cup olive oil
2 tablespoons chopped fresh rosemary, or
    2 teaspoons dried rosemary
2 or 3 garlic cloves, crushed
2 (12-ounce) pork tenderloins
freshly ground pepper to taste

Mix the orange juice, soy sauce, olive oil, rosemary and garlic in a shallow glass dish. Add the pork tenderloins to the orange juice mixture and turn to coat. Marinate, covered, in the refrigerator for 2 to 10 hours, turning occasionally.

Preheat the oven to 400 degrees. Drain the pork, reserving the marinade. Arrange the pork in a shallow baking dish and sprinkle with pepper. Roast for 20 minutes or to the desired degree of doneness. Bring the reserved marinade to a boil in a saucepan and boil for 2 minutes. Slice the pork and serve with the hot marinade if desired. In the winter, serve with a mixture of sautéed zucchini, onions and canned stewed tomatoes along with steamed new potatoes.

Grill the pork as an alternative. Sear the pork on all sides and grill, covered, until a meat thermometer inserted in the thickest portion registers 155 degrees. Serve with steamed fresh vegetables.

MEAT & GAME

Rosemary Pork Tenderloin

A real hit at tailgates, cocktail buffets, or company dinners.

YIELD: 8 SERVINGS

PORK MARINADE

Mix 1 cup extra-virgin olive oil, 1 cup chicken stock, 1/4 cup red wine, 1/4 cup balsamic vinegar, 1/4 cup minced shallots, 1/4 cup bread crumbs, 2 teaspoons melted butter, 1 teaspoon Worcestershire sauce, 1 teaspoon chopped fresh thyme, and salt and pepper to taste in a bowl and pour over pork tenderloins. Marinate in the refrigerator for about 2 hours. Grill or roast in the oven until a meat thermometer inserted in the thickest portion registers 155 degrees.

1/3 cup Dijon mustard
3 tablespoons maple syrup
2 tablespoons freshly
    ground pepper
1 tablespoon chopped
    fresh rosemary
3 garlic cloves, chopped
2 pork tenderloins
6 slices bacon
6 sprigs of rosemary

Combine the Dijon mustard, syrup, pepper, chopped rosemary and garlic in a bowl and mix well. Rub the mustard mixture over the surface of the tenderloins and wrap each individually in plastic wrap. Marinate in the refrigerator for 1 hour or longer.

Preheat the grill. Remove the plastic wrap and wrap each tenderloin with 3 slices of the bacon; secure with wooden picks. Insert 3 sprigs of rosemary into each tenderloin.

Grill over hot coals for 30 minutes or bake at 350 degrees for 45 minutes or to the desired degree of doneness. Slice and serve garnished with additional sprigs of rosemary.

COMPLIMENTS OF

Chinese Ribs

YIELD: 4 SERVINGS

2 racks of baby back ribs
peanut oil
Chinese five-spice powder to taste
1 cup soy sauce
1 cup fresh or canned grapefruit juice
1/4 cup ketchup
1/4 cup oyster sauce
1/4 cup packed light brown sugar
3 tablespoons rice wine vinegar
2 green onions, chopped
2 slices green chile

Preheat the oven to 300 degrees. Brush the surface of the ribs with peanut oil and sprinkle with five-spice powder. Arrange the ribs on a baking sheet and bake for 2 hours.

Combine the soy sauce, grapefruit juice, ketchup, oyster sauce, brown sugar, vinegar, green onions and green chile slices in a saucepan and simmer for 20 to 30 minutes, stirring occasionally. Strain the sauce into a bowl, discarding the solids.

Remove the ribs from the oven and brush liberally with the sauce. Bake for 15 to 20 minutes longer and serve.

YIELD: 18 SERVINGS

1½ pounds chorizo, casings
 removed and sausage sliced
3 pounds boneless skinless
 chicken breasts, chopped
1 pound pork, cut into
 bite-size pieces
1 teaspoon salt
1 onion, chopped
1 red bell pepper, chopped
1 green bell pepper, chopped
2 garlic cloves, minced
4 cups boiling water or
 chicken stock
2 (8-ounce) packages
 paella rice

2 tomatoes, peeled and
 chopped, or 1 (8-ounce) can
 stewed tomatoes
2 teaspoons salt
pepper to taste
1 (10-ounce) package frozen
 green peas
2 pounds shrimp, peeled
 and deveined
6 clams or crawfish in shells
 (optional)
1 (2-ounce) jar sliced pimento,
 drained

Preheat the oven to 375 degrees. Brown the sausage in a large skillet. Remove the sausage to a platter, reserving the pan drippings. Season the chicken and pork with 1 teaspoon salt and brown in the reserved pan drippings, stirring frequently. Remove the chicken and pork to paper towels to drain, reserving the pan drippings.

Add the onion, bell peppers and garlic to the reserved pan drippings and cook until the onion is tender but not brown. Stir in the boiling water, rice, tomatoes, 2 teaspoons salt and pepper. Bring to a boil and stir in the sausage.

Pour the rice mixture into a large baking pan or paella pan and spoon the chicken and pork over the top. Bake, covered, for 30 minutes. Rinse the peas in a colander with hot water to thaw and arrange the peas and shrimp over the top of the rice mixture. Top with the clams.

Bake, covered, for 15 minutes longer or until the chicken and pork are cooked through and the rice is tender. Garnish with the pimento. You may substitute a mixture of 2 cups uncooked rice and 3/16 teaspoon saffron for the paella rice.

COMPLIMENTS OF

YIELD: 50 SERVINGS

Baked Country Ham
1 whole ham
1 cup baking soda
2 to 3 magnums cabernet sauvignon,
    Coca-Cola Classic or apple cider
watercress

Jezebel Sauce
1 (10-ounce) jar orange marmalade
1 (4-ounce) jar prepared horseradish
1 (5-ounce) jar yellow mustard
5 tablespoons apple jelly

For the ham, rinse the ham and sprinkle with the baking soda. Scrub with a brush. Soak the ham in enough water to cover in a large nonreactive container for 24 hours. Drain and rinse.

Preheat the oven to 275 degrees. Place the ham in a roasting pan and pour the wine over the ham. Bake, covered, for 30 minutes. Reduce the oven temperature to 200 degrees and bake for 12 to 16 hours longer or until the ham is easily pierced with a meat fork. Remove to a serving platter and slice as desired. Garnish with watercress and serve with yeast rolls, Jezebel Sauce or Horseradish Sauce (page 115).

For the sauce, combine the marmalade, prepared horseradish, mustard and jelly in a bowl and mix well. Chill, covered, in the refrigerator.

MEAT & GAME

Sherried Veal Cutlets

YIELD: 4 SERVINGS

You can slice mushroom caps quickly and uniformly by using an egg slicer.

3/4 cup all-purpose flour
1/2 teaspoon salt
1/2 teaspoon pepper
1/8 teaspoon paprika
1 to 1 1/2 pounds veal cutlets,
    1/4 inch thick
2 tablespoons butter
2 tablespoons olive oil
1/2 cup sherry or madeira
1/3 cup teriyaki sauce
1/3 cup water
sliced fresh mushrooms
hot cooked rice

Mix the flour, salt, pepper and paprika and coat the veal with the flour mixture. Heat the butter and olive oil in a large skillet and add the veal. Cook until brown on both sides.

Mix the sherry, teriyaki sauce and water in a bowl and add to the skillet. Simmer for 20 minutes and stir in the mushrooms. Simmer for 20 minutes longer or until the veal is tender, stirring occasionally. Add additional water, wine or teriyaki sauce if the mixture becomes too dry. Spoon over hot cooked rice on a serving platter and serve with steamed fresh asparagus.

COMPLIMENTS OF

Veal Piccata

YIELD: 2 SERVINGS

1 pound veal scallops
all-purpose flour
1/4 teaspoon garlic powder
salt and pepper to taste
1/2 cup (1 stick) butter
1/2 cup white wine
2 tablespoons lemon juice
2 tablespoons drained small capers
2 tablespoons chopped fresh parsley
1 tablespoon chopped fresh
    tarragon, or 1/4 teaspoon
    dried tarragon
1 small lemon, thinly sliced

Dust the scallops with flour and sprinkle
with the garlic powder, salt and pepper.
Heat the butter in a large skillet and
add the veal. Sauté until cooked through.
Remove the veal to a platter, reserving the
pan drippings. Cover to keep warm.

Add the wine to the reserved pan drippings
and cook until slightly reduced, stirring
frequently. Stir in the lemon juice, capers,
parsley and tarragon. Cook until heated
through. Drizzle the sauce over the veal and
garnish with the lemon slices.

Grilled Veal Chops

YIELD: 6 SERVINGS

6 veal chops, 1 inch thick
garlic-flavor olive oil
herbs to taste
salt and freshly ground pepper
    to taste

Preheat the grill. Brush the surface of the
veal chops with olive oil and sprinkle with
the desired herbs.

Grill over hot coals for 4 minutes per side for
rare, sprinkling with salt and pepper when
the veal chops are turned. Serve immediately.

MEAT & GAME

YIELD: 4 SERVINGS

4 veal medallions
3 tablespoons all-purpose flour
salt and pepper to taste
$1/4$ cup ($1/2$ stick) butter or margarine,
    softened
2 teaspoons all-purpose flour
1 teaspoon water
$1/2$ cup white wine
$1/2$ cup chicken broth
1 tablespoon green peppercorns (optional)
1 teaspoon minced fresh ginger
grated zest and juice of 1 lime

Pound the veal between sheets of waxed paper to flatten. Mix 3 tablespoons flour, salt and pepper and coat the veal with the flour mixture. Heat the butter in a skillet over medium-high heat and add the veal.

Sauté for 1 to 2 minutes per side or to the desired degree of doneness. Remove the veal to a platter using a slotted spoon, reserving the pan drippings. Cover with foil to keep warm.

Mix 2 teaspoons flour and the water in a bowl until paste consistency. Add the wine and broth to the reserved pan drippings and bring to a boil, stirring with a wooden spoon to loosen any browned bits. Gradually whisk the flour mixture into the wine mixture.

Cook to a sauce consistency, stirring constantly. Stir in the peppercorns, ginger, lime zest and lime juice and cook just until heated through. Taste and adjust the seasonings. Return the veal to the skillet and turn to coat. Remove the veal to a platter with a slotted spoon and drizzle with the sauce. Serve immediately.

COMPLIMENTS OF

Osso Buco

YIELD: 6 SERVINGS

2 whole veal shanks, cut into
    2-inch pieces
salt and pepper to taste
all-purpose flour
1/2 cup olive oil
1 cup minced mild onion
2/3 cup minced carrots
2/3 cup minced celery
1/4 cup (1/2 stick) butter
2 teaspoons minced garlic
2 strips lemon zest
1 cup dry white wine

1 cup (or more) beef or veal stock
1 1/2 cups coarsely chopped
    canned Italian tomatoes
    with juice
1 teaspoon chopped fresh basil
2 bay leaves
3 sprigs each of thyme and
    parsley, or dried equivalent
1/4 cup minced fresh parsley
1 tablespoon grated lemon zest
3 garlic cloves, minced
parsley and lemon slices

Preheat the oven to 350 degrees. Have the butcher saw off the ends of the shanks with little meat. Leaving the skin intact, tie kitchen twine around each piece to prevent the meat from falling off the bone. Season with salt and pepper and coat with flour. Heat the olive oil in a skillet until hot. Sauté the veal in the hot oil until dark brown. Remove the veal to a platter using a slotted spoon, reserving the pan drippings.

Sauté the onion, carrots and celery in the butter in an ovenproof pan large enough to hold the veal in a single layer. Stir in 2 teaspoons garlic and 2 strips lemon zest. Remove from the heat and stand the veal vertically over the sautéed vegetables. Add the wine to the reserved pan drippings and bring to a boil, stirring with a wooden spoon to loosen any browned bits. Cook until the wine mixture is reduced by 1/2. Stir in the stock, tomatoes, basil, bay leaves, thyme and 3 sprigs of parsley and pour over the veal, adding additional stock if the liquid does not come to the top of the veal. Bring to a simmer and place the baking dish in the lower third of the oven.

Bake for 2 hours or until the veal is tender, turning and basting the veal every 20 minutes and adding warm water as needed for the desired consistency. The sauce should be thick and creamy. Remove the veal to a heated platter and discard the bay leaves. Taste the sauce and adjust the seasonings. Cook if needed for a thicker consistency. Stir in a mixture of 1/4 cup parsley, 1 tablespoon grated lemon zest and 3 minced garlic cloves or serve on the side. Spoon the sauce over the veal and garnish with sprigs of parsley and lemon slices.

YIELD: 4 SERVINGS

20 dove breasts
2 cups red wine
1 tablespoon cracked pepper
1/4 cup minced onion
1/4 cup (1/2 stick) butter
10 slices bacon, cut into halves
1/2 cup all-purpose flour
1 1/2 teaspoons coarse salt
1 teaspoon garlic powder
1/2 cup red wine
6 ounces small white mushrooms,
    thinly sliced
1 cup chicken bouillon
1/2 cup sour cream
hot cooked wild rice

Remove all shot and pinfeathers from the dove breasts and rinse with cold water. Place the dove breasts in a large sealable plastic bag and add 2 cups wine and the cracked pepper. Seal tightly and turn to coat. Marinate in the refrigerator for 8 to 10 hours, turning occasionally, or store in the freezer until ready to prepare.

Sauté the onion in the butter in a large skillet until tender. Drain the dove breasts and wrap each with 1 of the bacon pieces; secure with wooden picks. Combine the flour, salt and garlic powder in a sealable plastic bag and add the doves. Seal tightly and shake to coat.

Brown the doves on all sides in the skillet with the onion over medium heat. Add 1/2 cup wine and cook, covered, over low heat for 45 minutes. Stir in the mushrooms and cook for 45 minutes longer, adding the chicken bouillon as needed for moisture. Remove from the heat and stir in the sour cream. Serve over hot cooked wild rice.

Deadly Duck

YIELD: 4 TO 6 SERVINGS AS AN ENTRÉE,
OR 20 SERVINGS AS AN APPETIZER

3 or 4 whole duck breasts
$1/2$ cup Worcestershire sauce
$1/2$ cup zesty Italian salad dressing
1 tablespoon frozen lemon juice concentrate,
    or 2 tablespoons fresh lemon juice
1 tablespoon soy sauce
8 to 10 slices bacon, cut into halves

Debone the duck breasts and reserve the bones for preparing homemade stock. Cut the duck into 1- to $1^1/_2$-inch-thick strips. Combine the Worcestershire sauce, salad dressing, lemon juice concentrate and soy sauce in a bowl and mix well. Add the duck and turn to coat. Marinate, covered, in the refrigerator for 8 to 10 hours; drain.

Preheat the grill. Roll the duck strips into pinwheels and wrap each with bacon; secure with wooden picks. Grill over hot coals for 3 to 5 minutes per side.

....great harmonies can be produced by wonderful

food and music.

—*Beverly Sills*

YIELD: 4 SERVINGS

Beurre manié is a paste made of equal portions of softened butter and flour used to thicken gravy or sauces. Add to the gravy and cook to the desired consistency, stirring constantly.

6 to 8 quail
salt and pepper to taste
all-purpose flour
1/2 cup (1 stick) butter
2 cups sliced fresh mushrooms
1 cup madeira
1 cup consommé
1 rib celery, cut into quarters
6 to 8 thin lemon slices
chopped fresh parsley
hot cooked wild rice

Preheat the oven to 350 degrees. Sprinkle the quail with salt and pepper and coat with flour. Brown the quail on all sides in the butter in a skillet. Remove the quail to a baking dish using a slotted spoon, reserving the pan drippings.

Sauté the mushrooms in the reserved pan drippings. Stir in the wine and consommé and bring to a boil. Pour the mushroom mixture over the quail. Add the celery and lemon slices and sprinkle with parsley.

Bake, covered, for 1 hour or until the quail are cooked through. Discard the celery and lemon slices and serve with hot cooked wild rice drizzled with the sauce.

COMPLIMENTS OF

Béarnaise Sauce

YIELD: 1 CUP

2 green scallions
2 sprigs of parsley
2 tablespoons tarragon vinegar
1/4 cup (1/2 stick) butter
1 tablespoon soup stock
1/2 teaspoon salt
1/8 teaspoon paprika
4 egg yolks

Combine the scallions and parsley in a food processor fitted with a steel blade. Pulse until chopped. Combine the scallion mixture and vinegar in a sauté pan and simmer until the mixture is reduced by 1/2, stirring frequently. Stir in the butter, stock, salt and paprika and simmer.

Process the egg yolks in a food processor until thick and pale yellow. Strain the vinegar mixture, discarding the solids. Gradually add the vinegar mixture to the egg yolks, processing constantly until incorporated. Keep warm in the top of a double boiler. If you are concerned about using raw egg yolks, use eggs pasteurized in their shells, which are sold at some specialty food stores, or use an equivalent amount of pasteurized egg substitute.

Blueberry Sauce

YIELD: 6 CUPS

2 tablespoons butter
1 red onion, finely chopped
1 or 2 jalapeños, seeded
    and chopped
4 cups fresh or frozen blueberries
1/2 cup packed brown sugar
1/2 cup wine vinegar
1/2 cup ketchup
6 tablespoons Dijon mustard
1/4 teaspoon Tabasco sauce

Melt the butter in a saucepan and add the onion and jalapeño. Sauté until the onion is tender; do not brown. Stir in the blueberries, brown sugar, vinegar, ketchup, Dijon mustard and Tabasco sauce.

Simmer for 30 minutes, stirring occasionally. Let cool and purée in a food processor. Chill, covered, for up to 3 weeks. Serve with pork.

MEAT & GAME

Madeira Sauce

YIELD: 4 CUPS

1 garlic clove
1 small onion, cut into quarters
1 small carrot, coarsely chopped
1 rib celery, coarsely chopped
2 tablespoons butter
2 tablespoons all-purpose flour
2 tomatoes, cut into quarters
1 sprig of parsley
1 bay leaf
1/4 teaspoon freshly ground pepper
4 cups beef broth
1 cup madeira
salt to taste

Place the garlic in a food processor and pulse until minced. Add the onion, carrot and celery and pulse until minced. Brown the garlic mixture in the butter in a saucepan, stirring frequently. Add the flour and cook until thickened, stirring constantly.

Process the tomatoes, parsley, bay leaf and pepper in a food processor until chopped and add to the garlic mixture. Stir in the broth and simmer for 30 minutes, stirring occasionally. Strain into a bowl, discarding the solids. Stir in the wine and season to taste with salt.

Pineapple Chutney

YIELD: 3 OR 4 PINTS

4 cups syrup-pack crushed
    pineapple
2 cups raisins
1 cup cider vinegar
1 cup packed brown sugar
1/4 cup ground cinnamon
1/4 cup chopped candied ginger
4 garlic cloves, crushed
1 tablespoon salt
1/4 teaspoon cayenne pepper
1/4 teaspoon ground cloves
1/3 cup almonds

Combine the pineapple, raisins, vinegar, brown sugar, cinnamon, ginger, garlic, salt, cayenne pepper and cloves in a saucepan and mix well. Cook over low heat for 1 hour or until thickened, stirring frequently.

Stir the almonds into the pineapple mixture and spoon the chutney into 3 or 4 hot sterilized pint jars; seal with 2-piece lids. Serve with pork or chicken.

COMPLIMENTS OF

Horseradish Sauce

YIELD: 1 1/3 CUPS

1 cup mayonnaise
juice of 1 lemon
2 tablespoons grated onion
2 tablespoons prepared horseradish
1/2 teaspoon salt
1/8 teaspoon Tabasco sauce or
   cayenne pepper

Combine the mayonnaise, lemon juice, onion, prepared horseradish, salt and Tabasco sauce in a bowl and mix well. Store, covered, in the refrigerator.

Roasted Pepper and Artichoke Relish

YIELD: 4 SERVINGS

1 garlic clove, minced
1/2 teaspoon salt
1 1/2 teaspoons balsamic vinegar
1/4 teaspoon Dijon mustard
1/4 teaspoon pepper
1/4 teaspoon sugar
2 tablespoons olive oil
1 (6-ounce) jar marinated artichoke
   hearts, drained, rinsed and
   patted dry
1 (12-ounce) jar roasted red
   peppers, rinsed, patted dry and
   cut into thin strips
2 tablespoons chopped fresh basil
salt and pepper to taste

Mash the garlic with a pinch of the 1/2 teaspoon salt in a bowl. Whisk in the remaining salt, vinegar, Dijon mustard, pepper and sugar. Add the olive oil gradually, whisking constantly until incorporated. Coarsely chop the artichokes and add to the olive oil mixture. Stir in the roasted red peppers and basil and season to taste with salt and pepper. Serve with grilled steaks, pork and veal.

Seafood & Poultry

Thai Scallops and Asparagus *page 125*

YIELD: 4 SERVINGS

Sprinkle lime or lemon zest on fish for added flavor. It does not "cook" the fish as the juice does.

1½ to 2 pounds tilapia or catfish
  fillets, or whole fish
juice of 2 limes
1½ to 2 teaspoons salt
4 carrots, thinly sliced
1 small white onion, sliced
2 tomatoes, sliced
2 to 4 serranos, poblanos or
  jalapeños, seeded and
  chopped
¼ bunch cilantro, trimmed and
  chopped
lime wedges
sprigs of cilantro

Preheat the oven to 350 degrees. Arrange the fillets in a single layer in a shallow baking dish. Mix the lime juice and salt in a bowl and pour over the fillets, turning to coat. Toss the carrots, onion, tomatoes, serranos and chopped cilantro in a bowl and spoon over the fillets.

Bake, covered with foil, for 15 to 20 minutes or until the fillets flake easily. Remove the fillets to a serving platter and garnish with lime wedges and sprigs of cilantro. Serve with hot cooked rice.

The Best Baked Fish

YIELD: 6 SERVINGS

White Wine Marinade
1 cup dry white wine
1 teaspoon (rounded)
    Dijon mustard
1/4 cup soy sauce
1/4 to 1/2 garlic clove, minced

Fish
6 fish fillets such as tilapia,
    orange roughy, sole or salmon
1/2 cup (1 stick) unsalted butter,
    melted
1/2 teaspoon Worcestershire sauce
1/4 cup lemon juice
1/8 teaspoon Tabasco sauce
freshly ground black or
    white pepper
lemon slices
Chinese parsley

For the marinade, whisk the wine, Dijon mustard, soy sauce and garlic in a bowl until foamy.

For the fish, rinse the fillets with cold water and pat dry with paper towels. Place the fillets in a sealable plastic bag and add the marinade. Seal tightly and turn to coat. Marinate in the refrigerator for 30 to 60 minutes, turning occasionally; drain.

Preheat the oven to 450 degrees. Combine the butter, Worcestershire sauce, lemon juice and Tabasco sauce in a bowl and mix with a fork. Brush the skin side of the fillets generously with the butter mixture and arrange skin side down on a large baking sheet. Brush the remaining side with the butter mixture and sprinkle lightly with freshly ground pepper.

Arrange the baking sheet on the top oven rack and bake for 8 to 10 minutes. Brush the fillets with the remaining butter mixture and bake for 4 to 8 minutes longer or until the fillets are golden brown and flake easily. Remove the fillets to a serving platter and garnish with lemon slices and Chinese parsley. Broil the fillets if desired, but watch carefully as they will cook very quickly. You may substitute a mixture of 1/4 cup butter and 1/4 cup olive oil for the butter.

FISH STEAK MARINADE

Mix 1/4 cup olive oil, juice of 1 lime, juice of 1 lemon, 2 minced garlic cloves, 1 tablespoon chopped fresh basil, 1 teaspoon dried thyme, and salt and pepper to taste in a shallow dish. Add the desired fish steaks and turn to coat. Marinate in the refrigerator for 30 minutes; drain, reserving the marinade. Arrange the steaks on a grill rack sprayed with nonstick cooking spray and grill over hot coals until the steaks flake easily, turning and brushing with the reserved marinade occasionally.

Catfish
4 catfish fillets
juice of 2 lemons
all-purpose flour
olive oil or butter

Shrimp Sauce
juice of 1/2 lemon
8 ounces shrimp, peeled and deveined
2 tablespoons olive oil or butter
8 mushrooms, thinly sliced
2 whole scallions, finely chopped
1 tablespoon all-purpose flour
1 teaspoon chicken broth concentrate
1 cup hot water
1/2 cup white wine

For the catfish, arrange the fillets in a shallow dish and drizzle with the lemon juice, turning to coat. Marinate, covered, in the refrigerator for 2 hours. Coat the fillets with flour and sauté in olive oil in a skillet until the fillets flake easily. Cover to keep warm.

For the sauce, drizzle the lemon juice over the shrimp in a shallow dish. Marinate, covered, in the refrigerator for 30 minutes. Drain, reserving the liquid. Sauté the shrimp in the olive oil in a skillet until pink. Remove the shrimp to a bowl using a slotted spoon, reserving the pan drippings. Cool and cut the shrimp lengthwise into halves. Add the reserved liquid, mushrooms and scallions to the reserved pan drippings and sauté until the scallions are tender. Sprinkle the flour over the mushroom mixture and cook over medium heat for 5 minutes, stirring constantly. Mix the broth concentrate and hot water in a bowl and add to the mushroom mixture along with the wine. Increase the heat and cook until the mixture is reduced by 1/2, stirring constantly. Stir in the shrimp and drizzle over the catfish.

COMPLIMENTS OF

Zippy Baked Catfish

YIELD: 6 SERVINGS

Lemon Cream

1 cup light sour cream
2 tablespoons lemon juice
1 tablespoon chopped fresh parsley
$1/2$ teaspoon grated lemon zest
$1/4$ teaspoon salt

Catfish and Assembly

6 (6- to 8-ounce) catfish fillets or
    any whitefish fillets
$1/4$ teaspoon salt
$1/4$ teaspoon black pepper
$1^1/2$ cups panko or unseasoned bread crumbs
$1/4$ teaspoon garlic powder
$1/4$ teaspoon salt
$1/8$ teaspoon cayenne pepper
4 egg whites
orange slices or lemon slices
sprigs of parsley

For the cream, combine the sour cream, lemon juice, parsley, lemon zest and salt in a bowl and mix well. Chill, covered, in the refrigerator.

For the catfish, preheat the oven to 375 degrees. Sprinkle the fillets with $1/4$ teaspoon salt and the black pepper. Mix the bread crumbs, garlic powder, $1/4$ teaspoon salt and the cayenne pepper in a shallow dish. Whisk the egg whites in a bowl until frothy. Dip the fillets in the egg whites and coat with the bread crumb mixture. Arrange the fillets in a single layer on a wire rack sprayed with nonstick cooking spray. Place the rack on a baking sheet lined with foil. Lightly spray both sides of the fillets with nonstick cooking spray and bake for 20 to 25 minutes or until golden brown. Remove to a serving platter and garnish with orange slices or lemon slices and sprigs of parsley. Serve with the cream.

Fillet of Salmon Crusted with Green Olives

This unusual salmon dish is delicious served with a mixed green salad with Avocado Dressing (page 44) and Parmesan Rice Spoon Bread (page 153). For dessert, serve Pretty Peachy (page 184). An explosion of tastes and textures.

YIELD: 1 SERVING

1 salmon or grouper fillet
olive oil
pimento-stuffed green olives, sliced
sprigs of parsley

Preheat the oven to 325 degrees. Arrange the fillet skin side down in a baking dish sprayed with nonstick cooking spray and drizzle with olive oil. Sprinkle olives over and around the fillet.

Bake, covered with foil, for 15 minutes. Remove the foil and bake for 10 to 15 minutes longer or until the fillet flakes easily. Remove the fillet to a serving plate. Drizzle with the pan juices and sprinkle with the olives. Garnish with sprigs of parsley.

Thirty minutes before grilling salmon fillets, drizzle them with balsamic vinegar and sesame oil and sprinkle with seasoned salt. Grill the fillets over hot coals for seven minutes per side or until opaque.

COMPLIMENTS OF

Peanut and Sunflower Encrusted Salmon

YIELD: 2 SERVINGS

2 tablespoons dry-roasted peanuts
2 tablespoons salted sunflower seed kernels
2 salmon fillets
freshly ground pepper
2 tablespoons butter
2 tablespoons olive oil
fresh lemon juice
lemon slices

Coarsely grind the peanuts and sunflower seed kernels in a blender or food processor and spread the peanut mixture in a shallow dish. Coat the fillets with the peanut mixture and sprinkle with pepper.

Heat 1 tablespoon of the butter and the olive oil in a skillet over medium-high heat. Add the fillets flesh side down and cook for 3 to 4 minutes or until brown; turn. Cook for 8 minutes longer or until the fillets flake easily, adding the remaining 1 tablespoon butter and the desired amount of lemon juice about 1 minute before the end of the cooking process. Serve with yellow rice, fresh green beans and lemon slices.

Scalloped Oysters

1 pint oysters
2 cups cracker crumbs
$^1/_2$ cup (1 stick) butter, melted
$^1/_2$ teaspoon salt
$^1/_8$ teaspoon pepper
$^3/_4$ cup half-and-half
$^1/_2$ teaspoon Worcestershire sauce

Preheat the oven to 350 degrees. Drain the oysters, reserving $^1/_4$ cup of the liquor. Mix the cracker crumbs, butter and salt in a bowl.

Layer $^1/_3$ of the cracker crumb mixture and $^1/_2$ of the oysters in a greased $1^1/_2$-quart baking dish and sprinkle with $^1/_2$ of the pepper. Top with $^1/_2$ of the remaining cracker crumb mixture, oysters and pepper.

Whisk the reserved oyster liquor, half-and-half and Worcestershire sauce in a bowl until blended and pour over the prepared layers. Sprinkle with the remaining cracker crumb mixture and bake for 40 minutes. Serve with wild game or turkey and dressing. Double the recipe for a larger crowd.

Fish to taste right must swim three times—
in water, in butter, and in wine.

—*Polish Proverb*

COMPLIMENTS OF

Thai Scallops and Asparagus

YIELD: 4 SERVINGS

1$\frac{1}{2}$ pounds sea scallops
1 tablespoon cornstarch
1$\frac{1}{2}$ tablespoons olive oil
1$\frac{1}{2}$ teaspoons grated fresh ginger
2 garlic cloves, minced
8 ounces fresh asparagus, trimmed and
    cut into 2-inch pieces (2 cups)
$\frac{1}{2}$ cup chicken broth
1 tablespoon fresh lemon juice
1 tablespoon soy sauce
1 teaspoon chile purée with garlic sauce
2 tablespoons chopped fresh basil
$\frac{1}{2}$ teaspoon grated lemon zest
2 cups hot cooked rice
sprigs of basil
cherry tomatoes

Toss the scallops and cornstarch in a bowl. Heat the olive oil in a skillet over medium-high heat and add the scallops, ginger and garlic. Stir-fry for 4 minutes. Remove the scallop mixture to a bowl, reserving the pan drippings.

Add the asparagus, broth, lemon juice, soy sauce and chile purée to the reserved pan drippings and mix well. Cook for 2 minutes, stirring frequently. Return the scallops to the skillet and heat, covered, for 1 minute. Remove from the heat and stir in the chopped basil and lemon zest. Immediately spoon the scallop mixture over the rice on serving plates. Garnish with sprigs of basil and cherry tomatoes.

Photograph for this recipe on page 116.

CREOLE SEAFOOD SEASONING

Combine 2¹/2 tablespoons salt, 2¹/2 tablespoons paprika, 2 tablespoons granulated garlic or garlic powder, 2 tablespoons freshly ground black pepper, 1 tablespoon cayenne pepper, 1 tablespoon thyme, 1 tablespoon oregano and 1¹/2 teaspoons onion powder in a jar and seal tightly. Shake to mix.

2 tablespoons olive oil
24 shrimp, peeled and deveined
¹/2 cup chopped scallions
2 shallots, chopped
¹/2 cup white wine
¹/2 cup heavy cream
¹/2 cup (1 stick) butter
2 tablespoons coarse mustard
salt and pepper to taste
lemon juice to taste
hot cooked rice or corn
    bread squares
sprigs of parsley
lemon slices

Heat 1 tablespoon of the olive oil in a skillet and add the shrimp. Sauté for 5 minutes or until the shrimp turn pink. Remove the shrimp to a bowl using a slotted spoon, reserving the pan drippings.

Heat the remaining 1 tablespoon olive oil with the reserved pan drippings and add the scallions and shallots. Sauté until the scallions are tender and stir in the wine. Add the heavy cream and mix well.

Cook for 4 to 5 minutes or until the mixture coats the back of a spoon, stirring frequently. Reduce the heat to low and whisk in the butter. Whisk in the mustard; do not allow to boil. Season to taste with salt, pepper and lemon juice. Return the shrimp to the skillet and mix well. Spoon over hot cooked rice or corn bread squares on serving plates. Garnish with sprigs of parsley and lemon slices.

COMPLIMENTS OF

New Orleans Barbecued Shrimp

YIELD: 4 SERVINGS

1 cup (2 sticks) lightly salted butter
1 cup vegetable oil
$1/4$ cup paprika
4 bay leaves
2 teaspoons Italian seasoning
2 teaspoons chopped garlic
1 teaspoon lemon juice
$3/4$ teaspoon black pepper
$1/2$ teaspoon basil
$1/2$ teaspoon cayenne pepper
$1/2$ teaspoon oregano
$1/2$ teaspoon salt
2 pounds unpeeled shrimp

Heat the butter in a saucepan until melted. Stir in the oil, paprika, bay leaves, Italian seasoning and garlic. Mix in the lemon juice, black pepper, basil, cayenne pepper, oregano and salt and bring to a boil, stirring constantly. Reduce the heat to low.

Simmer for 8 minutes, stirring occasionally. Remove from the heat and let stand for 30 minutes. Pour the sauce into a baking dish and stir in the shrimp 20 minutes before serving.

Bake in a preheated 450-degree oven for 15 minutes or until the shrimp turn pink. Discard the bay leaves and ladle the shrimp mixture into individual pasta bowls. Serve immediately with a mixed green salad and hot crusty French bread for dipping.

SEAFOOD & POULTRY

SHRIMP AND CRAB BOIL

Add 1 sliced lemon, 1 finely chopped small onion, 2 crushed large bay leaves, 1 teaspoon peppercorns, 1/2 teaspoon crushed red pepper flakes and 1 garlic clove to 2 quarts boiling water and boil for several minutes. Add shrimp and boil until pink.

Greek Shrimp with Feta Cheese

YIELD: 6 TO 8 SERVINGS

2 onions, thinly sliced
1/2 cup olive oil
2 pounds tomatoes, peeled and
    coarsely chopped
2 teaspoons (or more) salt
1 teaspoon chopped fresh parsley
1/2 teaspoon freshly ground pepper
2 large garlic cloves, minced
1/2 teaspoon dried basil, or
    1 1/2 teaspoons julienned
    fresh basil
Tabasco sauce to taste
8 ounces peeled cooked large shrimp
4 cups hot cooked white or
    saffron rice
1/2 cup frozen peas, cooked and
    drained
8 ounces feta cheese, crumbled
sprigs of basil

Sauté the onions in the olive oil in a large saucepan until tender. Stir in the tomatoes, salt, parsley, pepper, garlic, dried basil and Tabasco sauce. Simmer, covered, for 1 hour, stirring occasionally. Add the shrimp and simmer for 5 minutes.

Combine the rice and peas in a bowl and mix well. Spoon the shrimp mixture over the rice mixture on serving plates. Sprinkle generously with the feta cheese and garnish with sprigs of basil.

You may substitute an equivalent amount of chopped drained canned tomatoes for the fresh tomatoes. Double the sauce recipe and freeze 1/2 of the sauce for future use, adding the shrimp just before serving.

COMPLIMENTS OF

Shrimp and Artichoke Bake

YIELD: 4 TO 6 SERVINGS

1 (14-ounce) can artichoke hearts, drained
1 pound shrimp, cooked, peeled and deveined
4$^{1}/_{2}$ tablespoons butter
4$^{1}/_{2}$ tablespoons all-purpose flour
$^{3}/_{4}$ cup milk
$^{3}/_{4}$ cup heavy cream
salt and pepper to taste
$^{1}/_{4}$ cup sherry
2 teaspoons Worcestershire sauce
2 tablespoons butter
4 to 6 drops of Tabasco sauce
1 teaspoon lemon juice
4 ounces mushrooms, sliced
$^{1}/_{2}$ cup (2 ounces) grated Parmesan cheese
paprika to taste
puffed pastry shells or hot cooked rice

Preheat the oven to 350 degrees. Arrange the artichokes in a buttered 2-quart baking dish and layer with the shrimp. Melt 4$^{1}/_{2}$ tablespoons butter in a saucepan and stir in the flour. Cook until bubbly and stir in the milk and heavy cream.

Cook until thickened and of a sauce consistency, stirring constantly. Remove from the heat and season to taste with salt and pepper. Stir in the sherry and Worcestershire sauce.

Heat 2 tablespoons butter, the Tabasco sauce and lemon juice in a skillet and add the mushrooms. Sauté until tender and spoon the mushroom mixture over the prepared layers. Top with the sauce and sprinkle with the cheese and paprika. Bake for 25 to 30 minutes or until bubbly. Serve over puffed pastry shells or hot cooked rice. You may substitute chopped cooked chicken for the shrimp.

SEAFOOD & POULTRY

YIELD: 5 TO 6 SERVINGS

1 tablespoon vegetable oil
8 ounces smoked sausage,
    chopped
1 green bell pepper, chopped
1 small onion, chopped
1 garlic clove, minced
2$^{1}/_{2}$ cups canned chicken broth
1 (14-ounce) can stewed
    tomatoes
$^{1}/_{2}$ (4-ounce) can diced green
    chiles, drained
1 bay leaf
1 teaspoon Worcestershire sauce

1 teaspoon celery salt
$^{3}/_{4}$ teaspoon chili powder
juice of $^{1}/_{2}$ lemon
cayenne pepper to taste
kosher salt to taste
black pepper to taste
1 (10-ounce) package frozen
    chopped okra
1$^{1}/_{4}$ pounds medium shrimp,
    peeled and deveined
hot cooked rice
chopped fresh parsley

Heat the oil in a large saucepan over medium heat and add the sausage, bell pepper, onion and garlic. Cook for 10 minutes or until the sausage is brown, stirring constantly. Stir in the broth, undrained tomatoes and green chiles.

Bring to a boil and reduce the heat to medium. Stir in the bay leaf, Worcestershire sauce, celery salt, chili powder, lemon juice, cayenne pepper, salt and black pepper and simmer, covered, for 40 minutes, stirring occasionally. Add the okra and mix well.

Cook for 20 minutes longer, stirring occasionally. Stir in the shrimp and cook until the shrimp turn pink, stirring occasionally. Discard the bay leaf and ladle over hot cooked rice in bowls. Sprinkle with parsley and serve with a mixed green salad and hot crusty French bread.

White Rémoulade Sauce

YIELD: 2 CUPS

1 cup mayonnaise
   (homemade preferred)
2 tablespoons Dijon mustard
1 tablespoon minced onion
1 tablespoon prepared horseradish
1 tablespoon vinegar
1 tablespoon minced fresh
   Italian parsley
1 teaspoon paprika
$1/2$ teaspoon herbes de Provence
$1/2$ teaspoon salt
$1/2$ teaspoon Worcestershire sauce
$1/4$ cup olive oil

Combine the mayonnaise, Dijon mustard, onion, prepared horseradish, vinegar, parsley, paprika, herbes de Provence, salt and Worcestershire sauce in a bowl and mix well. Add the olive oil gradually, whisking constantly until incorporated. Chill, covered, for 8 to 10 hours.

Serve with boiled shrimp, as a dressing for seafood salad or as a dip for chilled steamed asparagus. If the sauce is prepared with commercially prepared mayonnaise, add a small amount of fresh lemon juice for a more homemade flavor.

Mornay Sauce

YIELD: 3 CUPS

2 tablespoons butter
$1^1/2$ tablespoons flour
$1^1/2$ cups milk
$3/4$ cup (3 ounces) shredded
   Swiss cheese
$1/2$ cup (2 ounces) shredded
   Parmesan cheese
$1/8$ teaspoon cayenne pepper
salt and black pepper to taste

Melt the butter in a saucepan and whisk in the flour until blended. Add the milk gradually, whisking constantly. Stir in the Swiss cheese, Parmesan cheese, cayenne pepper, salt and black pepper and simmer over low heat until thickened.

Grilled Cornish Game Hens

YIELD: 8 SERVINGS

Roasted Red Pepper Boats (page 168), Lemon Nut Wild Rice (page 155), and Banana Cream Pie (page 240) complement this dish.

4 Cornish game hens
kosher salt to taste
freshly ground pepper to taste
3/4 cup stone-ground mustard
6 tablespoons Dijon mustard
6 tablespoons soy sauce
2 tablespoons Pickapeppa Sauce

Split the game hens into halves and remove the backbones. Press lightly to flatten and sprinkle with salt and pepper. Combine the stone-ground mustard, Dijon mustard, soy sauce and Pickapeppa Sauce in a bowl and mix well.

Brush each side of the game hens with some of the mustard mixture and arrange in a shallow baking dish. Marinate, covered, in the refrigerator for 2 hours or longer.

Remove the game hens from the refrigerator 30 minutes before baking. Preheat the oven to 375 degrees and bake for 30 minutes or until the juices run clear, turning once. Preheat the grill and arrange the game hens bone side down on the grill rack.

Grill for 5 to 10 minutes and turn. Grill about 10 minutes longer or until the skin is crisp. Serve with a spinach salad, corn and crusty French bread.

Chicken Under a Brick

YIELD: 4 SERVINGS

1 (3- to 4-pound) chicken
1/4 cup olive oil
kosher salt to taste
freshly ground pepper to taste

Butterfly the chicken. Remove the backbone and flatten the chicken. Heat the olive oil in a 12-inch skillet over medium heat and add the chicken skin side down. Place a 10-inch lid over the chicken and weight down with a brick. Cook for 12 to 15 minutes.

Remove the brick and lid and turn the chicken. Season to taste with salt and pepper and replace the lid and brick. Cook for 12 to 15 minutes longer or until cooked through. Let stand for 10 minutes before serving.

Deviled Chicken

YIELD: 8 SERVINGS

2 (2 1/2- to 3-pound) chickens, cut into halves
1/2 cup Dijon mustard
1/2 cup vegetable oil
1/4 cup lemon juice
1 tablespoon brown sugar
1 tablespoon grated onion
1 teaspoon Worcestershire sauce
1/2 teaspoon celery salt
1/2 teaspoon tarragon
1/2 teaspoon dry mustard
salt and pepper to taste

Brush the surface of the chickens with the Dijon mustard and arrange in 2 shallow 3-quart dishes. Chill, covered, for 8 to 10 hours.

Preheat the grill and allow the coals to die slightly. Combine the oil, lemon juice, brown sugar, onion, Worcestershire sauce, celery salt, tarragon, dry mustard, salt and pepper in a bowl and mix well.

Arrange the chickens skin side down on the grill rack and grill for 45 minutes or until cooked through, turning and basting with the oil mixture every 10 minutes.

Chicken Dijon

YIELD: 6 SERVINGS

6 whole chicken breasts,
    split and boned
2 cups heavy cream
1 cup loosely packed sliced
    mushrooms
1/2 jar Dijon mustard
1/3 cup chablis
1 teaspoon Worcestershire sauce
cayenne pepper to taste
salt and black pepper to taste

Preheat the oven to 550 degrees. Pound the chicken between sheets of waxed paper with a meat mallet until flattened. Combine the heavy cream, mushrooms, Dijon mustard, wine, Worcestershire sauce, cayenne pepper, salt and black pepper in a bowl and mix well.

Spoon 1/2 of the cream mixture into a shallow roasting pan and layer with the chicken. Top with the remaining cream mixture and bake for 12 minutes; do not overcook. You may substitute 12 boneless chicken breasts for the whole chicken breasts.

Tequila Lime Chicken

YIELD: 6 SERVINGS

1 cup fresh lime juice
1/2 cup tequila
1/2 cup fresh orange juice
1 tablespoon chili powder
1 tablespoon chopped garlic
1 jalapeño, seeded
    and chopped
2 teaspoons salt
1 teaspoon pepper
6 boneless chicken breasts with skin
lime wedges

Combine the lime juice, tequila, orange juice, chili powder, garlic, jalapeño, salt and pepper in a bowl and mix well. Place the chicken in a large sealable plastic bag and add the lime mixture. Seal tightly and turn to coat. Marinate in the refrigerator for 6 to 8 hours, turning occasionally.

Preheat the grill. Drain the chicken, discarding the marinade. Grill the chicken over hot coals until cooked through, turning once. Remove to a serving platter and garnish with lime wedges. Serve with a mixed green salad and corn pudding. You may substitute leg quarters or thighs with or without bone for the chicken breasts.

COMPLIMENTS OF

Brochettes of Chicken and Pineapple

YIELD: 8 TO 12 SERVINGS

Teriyaki Sauce

3/4 cup pineapple juice	2 teaspoons minced fresh thyme
6 tablespoons soy sauce	1 teaspoon minced fresh ginger
1/4 cup packed brown sugar	1 teaspoon minced garlic
1/4 cup dry sherry	1 teaspoon dry mustard
2 tablespoons honey	2 teaspoons cornstarch

Chicken

4 whole chicken breasts	1 pineapple, cubed
vegetable oil	1 whole pineapple with top

For the sauce, combine the pineapple juice, soy sauce, brown sugar, sherry, honey, thyme, ginger, garlic and dry mustard in a saucepan and bring to a boil, stirring occasionally. Mix the cornstarch with a small portion of the hot teriyaki sauce in a heatproof bowl and add to the saucepan. Cook until slightly thickened, stirring frequently.

For the chicken, chop the chicken into bite-size pieces, discarding the skin and bones. Combine the chicken with 1 cup of the sauce in a bowl and mix until coated. Marinate, covered, in the refrigerator for 2 to 5 hours, stirring occasionally; drain.

Preheat the grill and brush the grill rack with oil. Soak 8 to 12 bamboo skewers in water. Thread the chicken and cubed pineapple alternately onto the skewers and brush the brochettes with some of the remaining sauce. Grill for 10 minutes or until the chicken is cooked through, turning and basting frequently with the remaining sauce.

Place the whole pineapple upright in the middle of a serving platter. Pierce the pineapple with the skewers at strategic points and arrange any remaining skewers at the base. Great presentation for a cocktail party.

Hoisin Chicken Skewers

1/4 cup hoisin sauce
1 tablespoon sesame oil
1 tablespoon rice vinegar
1 teaspoon grated fresh ginger
2 boneless skinless chicken breasts,
    cut into 1-inch pieces
salt and pepper to taste
sesame seeds (optional)

Preheat the grill. Whisk the hoisin sauce, sesame oil, vinegar and ginger in a bowl. Reserve 2 tablespoons of the sauce. Add the chicken to the remaining sauce and mix until coated.

Thread the chicken pieces 1/2 inch apart onto skewers and sprinkle with salt and pepper. Grill over hot coals for 8 minutes or until cooked through and slightly charred, turning and brushing with the reserved sauce frequently. Remove from the grill and sprinkle with sesame seeds.

…the getting together, the being together is what counts…

the meal is the magnet.

Moroccan Chicken

YIELD: 6 TO 8 SERVINGS

Spicy Sauce
1 large jar tomato and cilantro salsa,
    or salsa of choice
1/2 salsa jar water
2 tablespoons honey
1 teaspoon ground cinnamon
1 teaspoon ground cumin
1 teaspoon curry powder
1 teaspoon garlic powder

Chicken
10 to 12 chicken tenders
olive oil
1/2 cup golden raisins
1 package garlic/olive oil couscous,
    prepared
1 cup sliced almonds

For the sauce, combine the salsa, water, honey, cinnamon, cumin, curry powder and garlic powder in a bowl and mix well. Chill, covered, for several hours. Taste and adjust the seasonings. You may prepare up to 1 day in advance and store, covered, in the refrigerator.

For the chicken, brown the chicken on all sides in olive oil in a skillet. Add the sauce and simmer for 20 to 30 minutes or until the chicken is cooked through, adding the raisins 10 minutes before the end of the cooking process.

Spread the couscous on a serving platter and spoon the chicken and sauce over the couscous. Sprinkle with the almonds and serve immediately.

Pasta & Grains

Spinach Fettuccini with
Smoked Salmon *page 144*

Fettuccini with Artichokes
and Green Peas

YIELD: 4 TO 6 SERVINGS

Pasta was not commonly eaten in the United States until the late nineteenth century. Thomas Jefferson became quite fond of it while serving as ambassador in Europe. In 1788, he sent his assistant to Naples to purchase a macaroni machine.

4 ounces spinach fettuccini or
    plain fettuccini
12 baby artichokes, or
    1 (9-ounce) package frozen
    artichoke hearts
3 leeks, sliced
2 garlic cloves, minced
2 tablespoons olive oil
1 (10-ounce) package frozen peas,
    thawed
3/4 cup chicken broth
1/2 cup snipped fresh
    Italian parsley
2 teaspoons chopped fresh mint
grated Parmesan cheese

Cook the pasta using the package directions. Drain and cover to keep warm. Sauté the artichokes, leeks and garlic in the olive oil in a skillet for 5 to 7 minutes, stirring frequently. Stir in the peas and broth and bring to a boil. Reduce the heat to low.

Simmer for 5 minutes, stirring occasionally. Toss the artichoke mixture, parsley and mint with the pasta in a large bowl. Sprinkle with cheese and serve immediately.

COMPLIMENTS OF

6 ounces spaghetti

2 tablespoons butter or margarine

1/3 cup grated Parmesan cheese

2 eggs, beaten

1 cup cottage cheese

1 pound ground beef or bulk pork sausage

1/2 cup chopped green bell pepper

1/2 cup chopped onion

1 (8-ounce) can diced tomatoes

1 (6-ounce) can tomato paste

1 teaspoon sugar

1 teaspoon oregano, crushed

1/2 teaspoon garlic salt

1/2 cup (2 ounces) shredded mozzarella cheese

Preheat the oven to 350 degrees. Cook the pasta using the package directions; drain. Combine the pasta, butter, Parmesan cheese and eggs in a bowl and mix well. Pat the pasta mixture over the bottom and up the side of a 10-inch pie plate. Spread the cottage cheese over the prepared layer.

Brown the ground beef with the bell pepper and onion in a skillet, stirring until the ground beef is crumbly and the vegetables are tender; drain. Stir in the undrained tomatoes, tomato paste, sugar, oregano and garlic salt. Cook just until heated through.

Spoon the ground beef mixture into the prepared pie plate and bake for 20 minutes. Sprinkle with the mozzarella cheese and bake for 5 minutes longer or until the cheese melts. You may substitute a mixture of ground beef and sausage for either the ground beef or sausage. Prepare in advance and store, covered, in the freezer. Bake just before serving.

Penne with Spicy Gourmet Sausage

YIELD: 6 TO 8 SERVINGS

A simple salad of romaine topped with Avocado Dressing (page 44), a basket of crusty bread, and Buttermilk Panna Cotta (page 238) for dessert completes the meal.

12 ounces penne
salt to taste
1 tablespoon minced garlic
1 shallot, minced
1 tablespoon olive oil
1 pound gourmet sausage
    (chicken, lamb or duck)
2 tablespoons paprika
$1/8$ teaspoon cayenne pepper
$1^{1}/2$ cups chicken stock
$1/2$ cup heavy cream or
    evaporated milk
$3/4$ cup (3 ounces) freshly grated
    Parmigiano-Reggiano cheese
3 tomatoes, seeded and chopped
3 green onions, thinly sliced
2 tablespoons julienned fresh basil
1 tablespoon minced fresh oregano
freshly ground black pepper to taste
basil chiffonade

Cook the pasta in boiling salted water in a saucepan until al dente. Drain and cover to keep warm. Lightly sauté the garlic and shallot in the olive oil in a 14-inch skillet. Add the sausage, paprika and cayenne pepper and cook until the sausage is no longer pink, stirring frequently. Stir in the stock and cook until the mixture is reduced by $1/2$. Add the heavy cream and cook until the desired consistency.

Add the hot pasta to the sausage mixture and toss to mix. Stir in the cheese, tomatoes, green onions, basil and oregano. Season to taste with salt and black pepper. Spoon into pasta bowls and garnish with basil chiffonade. Serve with a mixed green salad and crusty bread.

COMPLIMENTS OF

Picnic Pasta

YIELD: 8 SERVINGS

16 ounces vermicelli
5 boneless skinless chicken breasts,
    sautéed or grilled
1/2 cup olive oil
1/4 cup mayonnaise
1/4 cup lemon juice
3 tablespoons Cavender's seasoning
1 (8-ounce) can sliced black olives,
    drained
1 bunch green onions, chopped
grated Parmesan cheese
grape tomatoes
sprigs of parsley and/or basil

Cook the pasta using the package directions, omitting the salt; drain. Cut the chicken into 1-inch pieces. Combine the olive oil, mayonnaise, lemon juice and Cavender's seasoning in a bowl and mix well.

Toss the pasta, chicken, olives and green onions in a pasta bowl. Add the mayonnaise mixture to the pasta mixture and mix until coated. Sprinkle with cheese and garnish with cherry tomatoes and sprigs of parsley and/or basil. Serve at room temperature or chilled.

Thai Salad

YIELD: 6 SERVINGS

Peanut Dressing
1/3 cup creamy peanut butter
1/2 cup rice vinegar
1/4 cup fresh lime juice
1/4 cup chopped fresh cilantro
2 tablespoons apple cider vinegar
2 tablespoons grated fresh ginger
1 tablespoon each honey, soy sauce
    and molasses
1 teaspoon Tabasco sauce
2 garlic cloves, minced

Salad
6 ounces vermicelli, cooked and
    drained
6 boneless skinless chicken breasts,
    grilled, sliced and chilled
2 cups shredded bok choy
1 cup peanuts, toasted
1 cucumber, chopped
4 green onions, chopped
salt and pepper to taste

For the dressing, combine all the ingredients in a bowl and mix well.

For the salad, toss the pasta, chicken, bok choy, peanuts, cucumber and green onions in a bowl. Add the dressing and mix until coated. Season to taste with salt and pepper. Chill, covered, until serving time. You may substitute 1 1/2 pounds peeled and cooked shrimp for the chicken.

PASTA & GRAINS

143

Spinach Fettuccini with Smoked Salmon

YIELD: 6 SERVINGS

Making pasta, which simply means "paste" or "dough," is one of the earliest culinary inventions. Pasta was being made by the Etruscans in central Italy as early as 500 B.C.

1 (10-ounce) salmon fillet
1 cup fish stock or vermouth
2 tablespoons clarified butter
3/4 cup chopped seeded peeled tomatoes
1/4 cup chopped shallots
1 1/2 teaspoons minced garlic
4 teaspoons chopped fresh dill weed
1 teaspoon chopped fresh rosemary
salt and pepper to taste
1/4 cup heavy cream
6 green onion bulbs, chopped
10 ounces smoked salmon, flaked
1 pound snow peas
1 red bell pepper, julienned
2 tablespoons clarified butter
hot cooked spinach fettuccini or
    calamari fettuccini

Poach the salmon fillet in the fish stock for 5 minutes or until cooked through. Remove the salmon to a bowl, reserving the stock. Flake the salmon. Heat 2 tablespoons clarified butter in a skillet and add the tomatoes, shallots and garlic. Sauté for 2 minutes and stir in the dill weed and rosemary. Season with salt and pepper. Add the reserved stock and heavy cream to the tomato mixture and cook until the mixture is reduced by 1/2 or until it is of a syrupy consistency, stirring frequently. Stir in the green onions, poached salmon and smoked salmon. Cover to keep warm.

Sauté the snow peas and bell pepper in 2 tablespoons clarified butter in a skillet until the desired crispness. Spoon the salmon mixture over the fettuccini on serving plates and arrange the snow pea mixture by the pasta.

Photograph for this recipe on page 138.

COMPLIMENTS OF

Cheese Tortellini with Crawfish Sauce

YIELD: 2 TO 3 SERVINGS

7 ounces cheese tortellini
1 onion, finely chopped
2 garlic cloves, minced
$^1/_2$ cup (1 stick) butter
1 pound crawfish tails or peeled
    medium shrimp
1 cup heavy cream
$^1/_4$ to $^1/_2$ cup (1 to 2 ounces) grated
    Parmesan cheese
2 tablespoons chopped fresh parsley
3 or 4 drops of Tabasco sauce
lemon juice to taste
salt and freshly ground pepper
    to taste

Cook the pasta using the package directions. Drain and cover to keep warm. Sauté the onion and garlic in the butter in a skillet for 3 to 4 minutes. Stir in the crawfish and cook for 5 minutes longer, stirring frequently. Add the heavy cream, cheese, parsley, Tabasco sauce and lemon juice and mix well.

Cook until heated through, stirring frequently. Fold in the pasta and season to taste with salt and pepper. Serve immediately with additional Parmesan cheese, a green salad and crusty rolls.

Pasta Shrimp Spectacular

YIELD: 10 TO 12 SERVINGS

3 pounds shrimp, peeled and
    deveined
1$^1/_4$ cups (2$^1/_2$ sticks) butter, melted
1 tablespoon Worcestershire sauce
1 tablespoon pepper
1 tablespoon lemon juice
1 teaspoon salt
$^1/_2$ teaspoon basil
$^1/_2$ teaspoon thyme
$^1/_4$ teaspoon garlic powder
12 ounces thin spaghetti
8 ounces processed cheese, cubed

Preheat the oven to 350 degrees. Combine the shrimp, butter, Worcestershire sauce, pepper, lemon juice, salt, basil, thyme and garlic powder in a Dutch oven and mix well. Bake for 30 minutes or until the shrimp turn pink, stirring every 10 minutes.

Cook the pasta using the package directions; drain. Stir the pasta and cheese into the shrimp mixture and bake if needed to melt the cheese. Serve with a mixed green salad and French bread.

PASTA & GRAINS

What keeps pasta from sticking is not the oil added to the cooking water, but cooking it in a large quantity of water. Rinsing drained pasta removes the starches, which helps the sauce adhere to the pasta. Use reserved pasta water to thin sauces. Long ribbons, such as fettuccini or tagliatelle, are best for oil- and tomato-based sauces. Chunky pasta, such as penne or fusilli, are best for meat-based sauces.

1 tablespoon butter
1/2 cup finely chopped onion
1/4 cup finely chopped celery
1/4 cup finely chopped carrots
1 1/2 teaspoons tomato paste
1 cup dry red wine
1 (10-ounce) can beef consommé
1/8 teaspoon each thyme and pepper
1 tablespoon butter
8 ounces fresh mushrooms, sliced
1 tablespoon water
1 teaspoon cornstarch
1/8 teaspoon salt
8 ounces penne rigate, cooked and drained
sprigs of flat-leaf parsley

Heat 1 tablespoon butter in a medium skillet over medium-high heat and add the onion, celery and carrots. Sauté for 5 minutes and stir in the tomato paste. Cook for 2 minutes, stirring constantly. Mix in the wine and cook for 10 minutes or until most of the liquid evaporates, stirring frequently. Stir in the next 3 ingredients.

Bring to a boil and cook for 3 minutes or until the mixture is reduced to 1 cup, stirring frequently. Strain through a sieve into a heatproof bowl, discarding the solids. Cover to keep warm.

Heat 1 tablespoon butter in a saucepan over medium-high heat. Add the mushrooms to the hot butter and sauté for 5 minutes. Stir in the consommé mixture and bring to a boil. Reduce the heat to low and simmer for 5 minutes. Mix together the water and cornstarch and add to the sauce. Add salt and bring to a boil. Boil for 1 minute, stirring constantly. Toss the mushroom sauce with the pasta in a pasta bowl and garnish with sprigs of parsley. Serve with warm baguettes and red wine.

Penne with
Creole Shrimp Sauce

YIELD: 4 TO 6 SERVINGS

1¹/₂ pounds fresh shrimp, peeled
    and drained
2 teaspoons Creole seasoning
2 tablespoons butter
4 green onions, sliced
2 garlic cloves, minced
1¹/₂ cups cream
1 teaspoon hot red pepper sauce
¹/₄ cup chopped fresh parsley
12 ounces penne, cooked
¹/₂ cup (2 ounces) freshly grated
    Parmesan cheese

Toss the shrimp with the Creole seasoning
in a bowl. Heat the butter in a large skillet
over medium-high heat and add the shrimp.
Cook for 5 minutes or just until the shrimp
turn pink, stirring constantly. Remove the
shrimp to a bowl using a slotted spoon,
reserving the pan drippings.

Add the green onions and garlic to the
reserved pan drippings and sauté for 2 to
3 minutes or until the green onions are
tender. Reduce the heat to medium and stir
in the cream and hot red pepper sauce. Bring
to a boil and reduce the heat. Simmer for
8 to 10 minutes or until slightly thickened,
stirring constantly. Stir in the shrimp and
parsley. Toss the shrimp sauce with the pasta
in a bowl and sprinkle with the cheese.

Orecchiette with
Lentil Gravy

YIELD: 2 TO 3 SERVINGS

¹/₂ onion, chopped
1 garlic clove, minced
1 tablespoon olive oil
1 (15-ounce) can tomato sauce
¹/₂ cup chopped fresh tomato
¹/₄ cup lentils, drained and rinsed
¹/₄ teaspoon oregano
¹/₄ teaspoon basil
¹/₄ teaspoon thyme
¹/₄ teaspoon salt
¹/₈ teaspoon Tabasco sauce
hot cooked orecchiette

Sauté the onion and garlic in the olive oil in
a large skillet until the onion is tender. Stir
in the tomato sauce, tomato, lentils, oregano,
basil, thyme, salt and Tabasco sauce.

Simmer, covered, for 45 to 60 minutes or to
the desired consistency, stirring occasionally.
Spoon the lentil sauce over hot cooked pasta
on a serving platter.

The people of Genoa are credited with inventing pesto. It was named after the pestle used to crush the ingredients in a mortar.

Spaghetti with Red Pesto Sauce

YIELD: 6 SERVINGS

Red Pesto Sauce
20 pitted black olives (Italian,
    French or kalamata)
10 oil-pack sun-dried tomatoes,
    drained
6 tablespoons olive oil
1 large garlic clove, minced
1 tablespoon minced fresh
    rosemary, or 1 teaspoon
    dried rosemary
2 teaspoons minced fresh thyme,
    or $2/3$ teaspoon dried thyme
$1/2$ teaspoon crushed red
    pepper flakes

Pasta and Assembly
6 quarts water
16 ounces spaghetti
3 tablespoons sea salt
$1/4$ cup chopped fresh
    flat-leaf parsley
freshly grated Parmesan cheese

For the sauce, combine the olives, sun-dried tomatoes, olive oil, garlic, rosemary, thyme and hot red pepper flakes in a blender or food processor and pulse until of a coarse consistency.

For the pasta, bring the water to a boil in a stockpot. Add the pasta and salt and cook using the package directions until al dente; drain. Toss the hot pasta with $1/2$ cup of the sauce in a bowl, reserving the remaining sauce for future use. Add the parsley and toss again. Serve with freshly grated Parmesan cheese.

COMPLIMENTS OF

Bleu Cheese Pasta Sauce
1/2 cup crumbled bleu cheese
1 to 2 tablespoons milk
sliced kalamata olives

Quick Pasta Sauce
2 cups marinara sauce
1 cup ricotta cheese
1 1/2 ounces vodka

Pesto Sauce
8 cups fresh basil or arugula
1 cup olive oil
1 cup (4 ounces) grated
    Parmesan cheese
2 tablespoons pine nuts, toasted
2 tablespoons minced garlic
kosher salt to taste

For the bleu cheese sauce, heat the cheese in a saucepan until melted. Thin with the milk to the desired consistency. Toss the sauce and olives with hot cooked pasta in a pasta bowl and serve immediately.

For the quick sauce, heat the marinara sauce, cheese and vodka in a saucepan, stirring frequently. Toss the sauce with hot cooked pasta in a pasta bowl and serve immediately.

For the pesto sauce, combine the basil, olive oil, cheese, pine nuts, garlic and salt in a food processor and pulse until smooth. Toss the sauce with hot cooked pasta or serve as an accompaniment to chicken, meats or vegetables. Use as a marinade with vegetables and shrimp before grilling.

*The discovery of a new dish does more for human happiness
than the discovery of a new star.*

—*Anthelme Brillat-Savarin,* The Physiology of Taste

To cook perfect long grain rice, bring a large saucepan of water to a boil and add the rice. Boil for fifteen minutes or until tender; drain. If cooking rice in advance of serving time, reheat the rice by placing it in a heatproof colander over boiling water. Steam, covered, until hot.

1/2 cup olive oil or vegetable oil
1 small onion, chopped
8 ounces ground chuck
1 bay leaf, crumbled
1 cup long grain rice
4 cups boiling water, beef broth
    or chicken broth
salt and pepper to taste
grated Parmesan cheese

Heat the olive oil in a 2-quart saucepan and add the onion. Sauté until tender. Add the ground chuck and bay leaf and cook over medium heat until the ground chuck is brown and crumbly, stirring occasionally; drain. Stir in the rice and boiling water.

Simmer, covered, for 20 minutes or until the rice is tender and the water is absorbed. Season to taste with salt and pepper and spoon into a serving bowl. Sprinkle with Parmesan cheese.

Bacon Cheddar Shrimp over Rice

YIELD: 6 SERVINGS

4 or 5 slices bacon, chopped
2 garlic cloves, minced
1 tablespoon all-purpose flour
3/4 cup half-and-half
1 pound shrimp, cooked, peeled and deveined
1/2 cup (2 ounces) shredded Cheddar cheese
3 tablespoons chopped fresh parsley
2 tablespoons maple syrup
salt and pepper to taste
1/2 cup (2 ounces) shredded Cheddar cheese
hot cooked rice or noodles
sprigs of parsley

Cook the bacon in a skillet until brown and crisp. Remove the bacon to a bowl using a slotted spoon, reserving 1 tablespoon of the bacon drippings. Sauté the garlic in the reserved bacon drippings. Add the flour and stir until combined. Stir in the half-and-half and cook until thickened. Remove from the heat and stir in the shrimp, 1/2 cup cheese, the parsley, syrup, salt and pepper.

Preheat the broiler. Spoon the shrimp mixture into a 2-quart baking dish and sprinkle with 1/2 cup cheese and the bacon. Broil for 1 minute and spoon over hot cooked rice or noodles on serving plates. Garnish with sprigs of parsley.

Rice Ring with Shrimp Sauce

YIELD: 4 TO 6 SERVINGS

1¹/₂ cups rice
1 large onion, minced
4 slices bacon, chopped
2 large garlic cloves, minced
2 tablespoons butter
2 cups tomato juice
1 (6-ounce) can tomato paste
1 (4-ounce) can sliced mushrooms, drained
1 small green bell pepper, chopped
6 (or more) olives, sliced
1 teaspoon marjoram
1 teaspoon thyme
1 bay leaf
1 pound peeled cooked shrimp

Cook the rice using the package directions and spread evenly in a buttered 1-quart ring mold. Place the ring mold in a larger baking pan and add enough hot water to the baking pan to reach halfway up the side of the mold. Let stand, covered with foil, at room temperature, or place in a 350-degree oven for 30 minutes.

Sauté the onion, bacon and garlic in the butter in a saucepan. Stir in the tomato juice, tomato paste, mushrooms, bell pepper, olives, marjoram, thyme and bay leaf and simmer for 1¹/₂ hours, stirring occasionally. Discard the bay leaf. Reserve 6 of the shrimp and stir the remaining shrimp into the sauce.

Invert the rice mold onto a serving platter and spoon the shrimp sauce into the center. Arrange the reserved shrimp over the top. Or, simply spoon the shrimp sauce over hot cooked rice on serving plates, omitting the rice ring. Serve with a mixed green salad and hot crusty French bread.

COMPLIMENTS OF

Red Beans and Rice

YIELD: 10 TO 12 SERVINGS

1 pound dried red beans
1 ham bone
1 pound ham, chopped
1 large onion, chopped
2 ribs celery, chopped
1 large bell pepper, chopped
2 tablespoons minced garlic
6 cups water
1 (10-ounce) can diced tomatoes
    with green chiles
3 bay leaves
salt and cracked pepper to taste
hot cooked rice

Soak the beans in a bowl with enough water to generously cover for 8 to 10 hours. Drain and rinse the beans. Crack the ham bone with vise grips to allow the bone marrow to be released.

Sauté the ham, onion, celery, bell pepper and garlic in a stockpot until the onion is tender. Stir in the water, undrained tomatoes, bay leaves, salt, pepper, beans and ham bone and simmer for 1¹/2 hours or until the beans are tender, stirring occasionally. Discard the ham bone and bay leaves and spoon the beans over hot cooked rice in bowls.

Parmesan Rice "Spoon Bread"

YIELD: 6 SERVINGS

1¹/2 cups milk, chilled
1 cup cooked rice, chilled
³/4 cup water
¹/2 teaspoon salt
3 tablespoons butter, sliced
5 egg yolks, beaten
¹/2 cup (2 ounces) finely grated
    Parmigiano-Reggiano cheese
2 tablespoons minced fresh chives
¹/4 teaspoon pepper
5 egg whites
¹/16 teaspoon salt
chopped fresh parsley

Mix the milk, rice, water and ¹/2 teaspoon salt in a 3-quart saucepan. Simmer over low heat for 20 minutes or until very thick, stirring frequently. Remove from the heat and stir in the butter. Stir a small amount of the hot rice mixture into the egg yolks. Stir the egg yolk mixture into the rice mixture. Mix in the cheese and spoon into a heatproof bowl. Cool to room temperature and stir in the chives and pepper.

Preheat the oven to 350 degrees. Beat the egg whites and ¹/16 teaspoon salt in a mixing bowl at high speed until soft peaks form. Fold the egg whites into the rice mixture. Spread in a buttered 9-inch deep-dish pie plate and bake for 20 to 25 minutes or until golden brown. Garnish with parsley.

PASTA & GRAINS

Herbed Rice

1 cup long grain rice
3 tablespoons butter or margarine
1 (10-ounce) can chicken broth
1/2 cup boiling water
1/3 cup dry white wine
4 green onions, chopped
1/3 cup pine nuts, toasted
1 teaspoon dried basil
freshly ground pepper to taste
sprigs of basil

Preheat the oven to 350 degrees. Spread the rice in a Dutch oven and bake, covered, for 20 to 30 minutes or until golden brown. Add the butter and stir until melted. Maintain the oven temperature.

Heat the broth, boiling water and wine in a saucepan and stir into the rice mixture. Bake, covered, for 30 minutes longer or until the liquid is absorbed and the rice is tender. Stir in the green onions, pine nuts, dried basil and pepper. Garnish with sprigs of basil and serve immediately.

Wild Rice Casserole

2 cups wild rice, rinsed
1/2 cup vegetable oil
1 cup chopped onion
1 cup finely chopped celery
2 cups beef stock or beef consommé
1 cup button mushrooms
1/2 cup chopped green bell pepper
2 teaspoons salt
1 teaspoon bitters
1 teaspoon chopped fresh parsley

Soak the wild rice in enough tepid water to cover in a bowl for 1 hour or longer; drain. Heat the oil in a Dutch oven or heavy skillet and stir in the wild rice, onion and celery. Sauté for 2 minutes. Add the stock, mushrooms, bell pepper, salt, bitters and parsley and mix well.

Simmer, tightly covered, for 1 1/2 hours or until the rice is tender. Cool the rice mixture and store, covered, in the refrigerator for 8 to 10 hours. Spoon into a baking dish and bake at 350 degrees for 20 to 30 minutes or until heated through.

COMPLIMENTS OF

Lemon Nut
Wild Rice

YIELD: 8 SERVINGS

1 cup wild rice
3 cups chicken stock or
　　chicken broth
2 1/2 teaspoons grated lemon zest
1 tablespoon lemon juice
1 tablespoon butter or margarine
2 teaspoons grated lemon zest
1/2 cup chopped pecans, toasted
1/4 cup minced fresh parsley
3 tablespoons minced green onions
sprigs of parsley

Rinse the wild rice with hot water 3 times and drain. Bring the stock, 2 1/2 teaspoons lemon zest, the lemon juice and butter to a boil in a medium saucepan over high heat. Stir in the wild rice and reduce the heat.

Simmer, covered, for 1 hour or until the liquid is absorbed and the rice is tender. Stir in 2 teaspoons lemon zest, the pecans, minced parsley and green onions. Spoon into a serving bowl and garnish with sprigs of parsley. Serve with Cornish game hens (page 132), chicken or fish.

Winter Mint
Wild Rice

YIELD: 8 SERVINGS

4 cups chicken broth
2 cups wild rice, rinsed and drained
1 cup cooked long grain white rice
1 cup (1/4-inch pieces) celery
1 cup (1/4-inch pieces) onion
2 tablespoons canola oil
1 cup dried cranberries
1 cup pecan halves, toasted
1/2 cup chopped fresh mint, or
　　1/4 cup dried mint
1 tablespoon freshly grated orange zest
1 teaspoon thyme
salt and pepper to taste

Bring the broth to a boil in a saucepan over high heat. Add the wild rice to the hot broth and reduce the heat to medium-low. Cook for 40 minutes or until the wild rice is tender, adding additional broth as needed; drain. Mix the wild rice and white rice in a bowl and cover to keep warm.

Sauté the celery and onion in the canola oil in a skillet for 5 minutes. Stir in the remaining ingredients. Prepare in advance and store, covered, in the refrigerator. Spoon into a baking dish and reheat, covered with foil, in a preheated 350-degree oven for 15 to 20 minutes.

Photograph for this recipe on page 92.

Mushroom Risotto

YIELD: 8 SERVINGS

12 medium mushrooms
6 to 8 cups beef stock
8 tablespoons unsalted butter
1 white onion, halved and sliced
2 cups arborio rice
3/4 cup pinot grigio or other white wine
3/4 cup (3 ounces) grated
    grana cheese
2 tablespoons chopped fresh parsley

Remove the stems from the mushroom caps, reserving the stems. Cut the caps into thin slices. Combine the reserved stems and stock in a saucepan and simmer for 30 minutes; maintain the stock on a low simmer. Heat 6 tablespoons of the butter in a saucepan and add the onion. Cook until the onion is tender, stirring constantly. Add the rice and stir until coated. Stir in the wine and cook until the wine evaporates.

Add the warm stock mixture to the rice mixture 1 cup at a time, cooking until the stock is absorbed after each addition and the rice is partially done, stirring constantly. Fold the sliced mushrooms into the rice and continue adding the warm stock mixture 1 cup at a time. Cook until the broth is absorbed after each addition and the rice is al dente, stirring constantly. Remove from the heat and stir in the cheese, parsley and remaining 2 tablespoons butter.

Risotto with Sausage

YIELD: 6 SERVINGS

1 teaspoon rosemary
6 to 8 cups chicken stock
3 tablespoons butter
Freshly ground pepper to taste
1 white onion, thinly sliced
2 cups arborio rice
1 pound Italian sausage,
    casings removed
1 cup red wine
1 teaspoon dry rubbed sage
3/4 cup (3 ounces) grated
    Parmesan cheese
1 tablespoon butter

Soak the rosemary in hot water in a bowl for 1 hour; drain. Bring the stock to a boil in a saucepan over high heat and reduce to a low simmer. Keep the stock warm over low heat. Heat 3 tablespoons butter in a Dutch oven. Add the pepper and onion and sauté until the onion is tender. Stir in the rice and sausage and sauté until the sausage is brown and cooked through. Add the wine and cook until the wine evaporates, stirring constantly.

Add the warm stock to the rice mixture 1 ladleful at a time and cook until the stock is absorbed after each addition and the rice is al dente, stirring constantly. Fold in the rosemary and sage. Remove from the heat and stir in the cheese and 1 tablespoon butter. Let stand, covered, for 2 to 3 minutes before ladling into bowls.

COMPLIMENTS OF

Gourmet Gruyère Grits

YIELD: 8 SERVINGS

2 cups half-and-half
2 cups milk
$^1/_2$ cup (1 stick) butter, sliced
1 cup grits
1 egg, beaten
1 teaspoon salt
$^1/_4$ teaspoon black pepper
$^1/_4$ teaspoon white pepper
$^1/_3$ cup butter, sliced
4 ounces Gruyère cheese, grated
$^1/_2$ cup (2 ounces) freshly grated
  Parmesan cheese

Preheat the oven to 350 degrees. Bring the half-and-half and milk to a boil in a saucepan, stirring frequently. Stir in $^1/_2$ cup butter and the grits and cook for 5 minutes or until thickened, stirring constantly. Remove from the heat and cool slightly. Add the egg, salt, black pepper and white pepper and mix until incorporated.

Stir $^1/_3$ cup butter and the Gruyère cheese into the grits mixture and spoon into a greased 2-quart baking dish. Sprinkle with the Parmesan cheese and bake for 1 hour. Serve immediately. You may prepare in advance and store, covered, in the refrigerator. Bake just before serving.

After a good dinner, one can forgive anybody,
even one's own relations.

—Oscar Wilde

Vegetables & Sides

Roasted Asparagus with
Pine Nuts *page 160*

Roasted Asparagus with Pine Nuts

YIELD: 12 SERVINGS

$1/3$ cup pine nuts
4 pounds fresh asparagus
3 tablespoons olive oil
1 teaspoon salt
$1/2$ teaspoon minced garlic
$1/4$ teaspoon pepper
2 ounces Parmesan cheese, shaved

Preheat the oven to 325 degrees. Spread the pine nuts on a baking sheet and toast for 10 to 15 minutes or until golden brown, stirring occasionally. Or, spread the pine nuts on a microwave-safe plate and microwave on High for 2 to $2^1/2$ minutes or until golden brown, stirring every 30 seconds. Increase the oven temperature to 425 degrees.

Line a roasting pan with foil. Snap off the thick woody ends of the asparagus spears and toss the spears with the olive oil, salt, garlic and pepper in the roasting pan. Roast for 5 to 10 minutes or until the asparagus is tender-crisp, turning once. Remove the asparagus to a serving platter and sprinkle with the pine nuts and cheese. Serve immediately.

Photograph for this recipe on page 158.

Marinated Asparagus

YIELD: VARIABLE SERVINGS

1 teaspoon salt
$1/4$ teaspoon paprika
$1/8$ teaspoon freshly ground
    black pepper
cayenne pepper to taste
$1/2$ cup olive oil
3 tablespoons wine vinegar
1 tablespoon grated onion
$1^1/2$ teaspoons chopped
    fresh parsley
$1^1/2$ teaspoons chopped fresh chives
fresh asparagus spears, trimmed
    and steamed
Bibb lettuce

Mix the salt, paprika, black pepper and cayenne pepper in a bowl. Add the olive oil and vinegar alternately, whisking constantly until incorporated. Stir in the onion, parsley and chives.

Pour the dressing into a jar with a tight-fitting lid and chill for 2 to 3 hours to allow the flavors to meld. Drizzle over asparagus on a serving platter. Marinate in the refrigerator for 2 hours or longer. Serve on a bed of Bibb lettuce.

COMPLIMENTS OF

Haricot Vert Sauté

YIELD: VARIABLE SERVINGS

4 cups water
haricots verts or very thin
    green beans
1 to 2 tablespoons unsalted butter
kosher salt to taste
freshly ground pepper to taste

Bring the water to a boil in a saucepan and add the beans. Cook for 3 to 5 minutes or until tender-crisp. Drain and immediately place the beans in a bowl of ice water to stop the cooking process. Drain and pat dry with paper towels

Heat the butter in a skillet and add the beans, salt and pepper. Sauté just until heated through and serve immediately.

Broccolini Italian-Style

YIELD: 3 TO 4 SERVINGS

4 cups water
1 bunch broccolini, trimmed
2 tablespoons extra-virgin olive oil
1/4 teaspoon minced garlic
kosher salt to taste
freshly ground pepper to taste

Bring the water to a boil in a saucepan and add the broccolini. Cook for 3 to 4 minutes. Drain and immediately place the broccolini in a bowl of ice water to stop the cooking process. Drain and pat dry with paper towels.

Heat the olive oil and garlic in a skillet and add the broccolini, tossing to coat. Cook just until heated through. Season to taste with salt and pepper and serve immediately.

How luscious lies the pea within the pod.

—*Emily Dickinson*

VEGETABLES & SIDES

Szechuan Broccoli

ARTICHOKES WITH BLEU CHEESE

Pour 1 drained 14-ounce can of artichoke hearts into a saucepan and crumble bleu cheese over the top. Cook just until heated through. You may substitute English peas for the artichokes. Great accompaniment with steaks and chicken.

2 tablespoons soy sauce
2 tablespoons rice wine vinegar
1 teaspoon sugar
4 teaspoons vegetable oil
3 garlic cloves, minced
1 teaspoon crushed red pepper
1 teaspoon grated fresh ginger
5 cups broccoli crowns,
    cut into halves
2 tablespoons sesame seeds,
    toasted

Heat the soy sauce, vinegar and sugar in a saucepan, stirring occasionally. Stir in the oil, garlic, red pepper and ginger and heat for 30 seconds. Add the broccoli and cook for 2 minutes or just until heated through and coated with the sauce, stirring frequently; do not overcook. Sprinkle with the sesame seeds and serve immediately.

COMPLIMENTS OF

Grilled Corn with Chipotle Butter

YIELD: 6 SERVINGS

Chipotle Butter
1/2 cup (1 stick) butter, softened
2 tablespoons chipotle hot sauce
1/2 teaspoon salt
1/4 teaspoon pepper
1/4 teaspoon garlic powder

Grilled Corn
6 ears of unhusked corn

For the butter, combine the butter, hot sauce, salt, pepper and garlic powder in a bowl and mix well. Chill, covered, in the refrigerator.

For the corn, pull the corn husks back, leaving the husks attached at the base of the cobs; remove the silk. Coat the corn kernels with some of the chilled butter and reposition the husks. Chill for 30 minutes or longer.

Soak the ears in cold water for 30 minutes; drain. Grill the corn over medium-hot coals for 30 minutes, turning occasionally. To serve, pull the husks back and tie at the base to form a handle. Store the remaining butter in the refrigerator for future use.

"The Best" Corn Pudding

YIELD: 12 SERVINGS

1 cup finely chopped onion
$1/4$ cup ($1/2$ stick) butter
5 cups fresh corn kernels
(about 8 ears)
$1/8$ to $1/4$ teaspoon sugar
salt and black pepper to taste
4 eggs, beaten
$1/2$ cup stone-ground
yellow cornmeal
1 cup milk
1 cup half-and-half
1 cup ricotta cheese
$1/2$ cup (2 ounces) shredded
Cheddar cheese
3 tablespoons chopped fresh basil
2 teaspoons salt
$3/4$ teaspoon white pepper
$1/4$ teaspoon Tabasco sauce
$1/2$ cup (2 ounces) shredded Cheddar cheese
paprika (optional)

Preheat the oven to 375 degrees. Sauté the onion in the butter in a large skillet for 3 to 5 minutes or until tender. Stir in the corn and sugar and season to taste with salt and pepper. Cook for 10 minutes, stirring occasionally. Mix the eggs and cornmeal in a bowl and stir in the milk, half-and-half and ricotta cheese. Stir in in the corn mixture, $1/2$ cup Cheddar cheese, the basil, 2 teaspoons salt, the white pepper and Tabasco sauce into the egg mixture.

Spoon the corn mixture into a greased 3-quart baking dish or a 9×13-inch baking dish and sprinkle with $1/2$ cup Cheddar cheese. Place the baking dish in a larger baking pan and add enough hot water to the baking pan to reach halfway up the sides of the baking dish. Bake for 40 to 45 minutes or until brown and bubbly. Sprinkle with paprika and serve immediately.

COMPLIMENTS OF

Mushroom Onion Gratin

YIELD: 6 SERVINGS

1 pound mushrooms, thinly sliced
2 1/2 tablespoons unsalted butter
1/4 cup all-purpose flour
2 large onions, thinly sliced
1 1/2 tablespoons unsalted butter
salt and pepper to taste
6 tablespoons heavy cream
1 cup (4 ounces) grated
    Gruyère cheese
1/4 cup fine fresh bread crumbs
chopped fresh parsley or chives

Preheat the oven to 325 degrees. Cook the mushrooms in 2 1/2 tablespoons butter in a skillet over medium-low heat until tender and most of the liquid has evaporated, stirring constantly. Stir in the flour and cook for 3 minutes, stirring constantly.

Layer 1/2 of the onions, 1 1/2 tablespoons butter, the mushroom mixture, salt, pepper and remaining onions in a baking pan or 6 gratin dishes. Pour the heavy cream evenly over the top and sprinkle with a mixture of the cheese and bread crumbs.

Arrange the baking pan on the center oven rack and bake for 50 to 60 minutes or until the onions are tender and the top is golden brown. Garnish with parsley or chives.

Onion Patties

YIELD: 3 DOZEN PATTIES

vegetable oil
3/4 cup all-purpose flour
2 tablespoons minced fresh parsley
1 tablespoon yellow cornmeal
1 tablespoon sugar
2 teaspoons baking powder
2 teaspoons dried sage
1 teaspoon salt
3/4 cup milk
3 drops of Tabasco sauce
2 1/2 cups finely chopped onions

Pour enough oil into a skillet to measure about 1 inch and heat to 360 to 380 degrees. Combine the flour, parsley, cornmeal, sugar, baking powder, sage and salt in a bowl. Stir in the milk, Tabasco sauce and onions.

Drop the onion mixture by tablespoonfuls into the hot oil and press lightly. Cook until brown on both sides, turning once; drain. You may prepare in advance and keep warm in a 225-degree oven for up to 1 hour.

VEGETABLES & SIDES

ROASTED GRAPE
TOMATOES

Heavily coat the bottom of
a baking dish with olive oil.
Add 2 pints grape tomatoes to
the prepared baking dish and
turn to coat. Sprinkle with
kosher salt, freshly ground
pepper and chopped fresh
basil and roast at 350 degrees
for 15 minutes.

Cracker Crust
1 1/2 cups soda cracker crumbs
1/4 cup (1/2 stick) butter, melted

Onion Filling
2 cups sliced Vidalia or sweet
    Walla Walla onions
2 tablespoons butter
3/4 cup milk
1 cup (4 ounces) shredded sharp
    Cheddar cheese
2 eggs, beaten
3/4 teaspoon salt
3/4 teaspoon pepper
paprika to taste

For the crust, toss the cracker crumbs with the butter in a bowl.
Pat the crumb mixture over the bottom and up the side of a 9-inch
pie plate.

For the filling, preheat the oven to 350 degrees. Sauté the onions in
the butter in a skillet until tender. Spread the onions in the prepared
pie plate. Whisk the milk, cheese, eggs, salt and pepper in a bowl
until mixed and pour over the onions. Sprinkle with paprika and
bake for 30 minutes.

COMPLIMENTS OF

Potato Gâteau Gratin

YIELD: 8 SERVINGS

1 garlic clove
lightly salted butter
2 egg yolks
2 teaspoons salt, or to taste
2 teaspoons freshly ground black pepper, or to taste
1/8 teaspoon cayenne pepper, or to taste
3 tablespoons chopped fresh herbs, such as Italian
   parsley, thyme and/or rosemary
2 cups heavy cream
8 ounces Gruyère cheese, grated
2 1/4 pounds potatoes, thinly sliced
3 tablespoons lightly salted butter, sliced
fresh herbs

Preheat the oven to 325 degrees. Rub the inside surfaces of a loaf pan with the garlic and coat generously with butter. Beat the egg yolks, salt, black pepper and cayenne pepper in a mixing bowl. Mix in 3 tablespoons chopped herbs. Add the heavy cream and 1/3 of the cheese and beat until incorporated.

Dip each potato slice in the cream mixture and arrange in an overlapping fashion in the prepared loaf pan until the potatoes fill the pan halfway, sprinkling some of the remaining cheese between each layer. Press the layers down with the back of a spoon and continue the layering process until the potatoes come to within 1/2 inch of the top of the pan. Pour the remaining cream mixture over the top, sprinkle with the remaining cheese and dot with 3 tablespoons butter. Place the loaf pan in a larger baking pan and add enough hot water to the baking pan to reach halfway up the sides of the loaf pan.

Bake, covered with waxed paper, for 1 1/2 hours. The gratin is done when a sharp knife inserted in the center comes out covered with smooth creamy potato. Turn off the oven and remove the waxed paper. Let the gratin stand in the oven with the door closed for 15 minutes to allow the top to brown and crisp. Invert onto a serving platter and garnish with additional fresh herbs.

Roasted Red Pepper Boats

YIELD: 8 SERVINGS

4 red bell peppers, cut into halves,
    stemmed and seeded
1 tablespoon olive oil
8 cups water
4 red potatoes
$1^1/_2$ teaspoons salt
$1^1/_2$ teaspoons dried thyme
1 teaspoon dried rosemary
$3/_4$ cup olive oil
$1/_4$ cup balsamic vinegar
$1/_2$ teaspoon salt
freshly ground pepper
6 ounces chèvre, crumbled
2 tablespoons finely chopped fresh parsley
    or chives
sprigs of parsley

Preheat the oven to 500 degrees. Line a baking sheet with foil and arrange the bell peppers cut side down on the foil. Brush the bell peppers with 1 tablespoon olive oil. Roast on the center oven rack for 8 to 10 minutes or until tender and slightly blistered. Set aside. Reduce the oven temperature to 375 degrees.

Bring the water to a boil in a saucepan and add the potatoes and $1^1/_2$ teaspoons salt. Boil for 25 to 30 minutes or until tender; drain. Cool, peel and cut into $1/_2$-inch pieces. Gently toss the potatoes with the thyme and rosemary in a bowl.

Whisk $3/_4$ cup olive oil, the vinegar, $1/_2$ teaspoon salt and pepper in a bowl until blended. Reserve 2 tablespoons of the vinaigrette. Pour the remaining vinaigrette over the potato mixture and toss to coat. Add the chèvre and mix well. Taste and adjust the seasonings.

Spoon the potato mixture evenly into the bell pepper shells. Arrange the bell pepper shells filling side up on a baking sheet and drizzle with the reserved vinaigrette. Bake on the center oven rack for 10 minutes. Sprinkle with chopped parsley and arrange on a serving platter. Garnish with sprigs of parsley and serve immediately.

Spinach Timbales

YIELD: 15 SERVINGS

1 (10-ounce) package frozen
    spinach, thawed and drained
2 or 3 green onions, sliced
3 tablespoons butter
1/2 cup herb-seasoned stuffing mix
1/2 cup (2 ounces) grated
    Parmesan cheese
1/3 cup mayonnaise
2 eggs, beaten
1/4 teaspoon garlic powder
1/8 teaspoon cayenne pepper
15 tomato halves
grated Parmesan cheese

Preheat the oven to 350 degrees. Press the excess moisture from the spinach. Sauté the green onions in the butter in a skillet until tender. Mix the spinach, green onions and the next 6 ingredients in a bowl. Shape the spinach mixture into rounds the size of the cut side of the tomatoes.

Arrange the tomato halves cut side up on a baking sheet and top each with a spinach round. Sprinkle with additional cheese and bake for 30 minutes or until the tomatoes are heated through and the spinach is brown.

You may prepare the spinach mixture in advance, shape into rounds and freeze for future use. Blanch fresh spinach before sautéing; then drain and pat dry. This emphasizes flavor, texture and color.

Sauerkraut Relish

YIELD: 4 CUPS

1 (20-ounce) can chopped
    sauerkraut
1 cup chopped onion
1 cup chopped celery
1 cup chopped bell pepper
1 cup sugar
1 cup vinegar

Combine the undrained sauerkraut, onion, celery and bell pepper in a heatproof bowl and mix well. Mix the sugar and vinegar in a saucepan and bring to a boil, stirring occasionally.

Pour the hot vinegar mixture over the sauerkraut mixture and mix well. Chill, covered, in the refrigerator. Serve with roast pork.

VEGETABLES & SIDES

Summer Squash Casserole

YIELD: 6 SERVINGS

MINT PESTO

Process 8 cups fresh mint,

1 cup olive oil, 1 cup grated

Parmesan cheese, 2 tablespoons

minced garlic and 1 tablespoon

toasted pine nuts in a food

processor or blender to the

desired consistency. Toss with

your favorite pasta.

$^1\!/2$ cup finely chopped onion
$^1\!/4$ cup chopped red bell pepper
$^1\!/4$ cup ($^1\!/2$ stick) butter
6 large yellow squash, sliced,
    steamed and drained
1 cup (4 ounces) shredded sharp
    Cheddar cheese
1 (8-ounce) can water chestnuts,
    drained
$^1\!/2$ cup mayonnaise
1 egg, beaten
1 teaspoon salt
1 cup dry bread crumbs

Preheat the oven to 350 degrees. Sauté the onion and bell pepper in the butter in a saucepan until tender. Stir in the squash, cheese, water chestnuts, mayonnaise, egg and salt.

Spoon the squash mixture into a buttered 1$^1\!/2$-quart baking dish and sprinkle with the bread crumbs. Bake for 30 minutes. Double the recipe for a larger crowd.

COMPLIMENTS OF

Sweet Potatoes with Sage Vinaigrette

YIELD: 8 SERVINGS

Sage Vinaigrette

3 tablespoons Champagne
    vinegar
2 tablespoons chopped
    fresh sage
1 tablespoon sugar
1 teaspoon salt
1/2 teaspoon pepper
1/3 cup olive oil
2 tablespoons dark sesame oil

Sweet Potatoes and Assembly

8 cups chopped peeled sweet
    potatoes (about 4 large
    sweet potatoes)
2 tablespoons olive oil
1 bunch green onions, trimmed
    and diagonally sliced
1 tablespoon sesame seeds
fresh sage leaves

For the vinaigrette, whisk the vinegar, sage, sugar, salt and pepper in a bowl. Add the olive oil and sesame oil gradually, whisking constantly until incorporated.

For the sweet potatoes, preheat the oven to 450 degrees. Line a 10×15-inch baking sheet with foil and coat with nonstick cooking spray. Toss the sweet potatoes with the olive oil in a bowl and spread in a single layer on the prepared baking sheet; do not allow the sides of the sweet potatoes to touch. Bake for 30 to 40 minutes or until tender.

Remove the sweet potatoes to a serving bowl and mix with the green onions and sesame seeds. Pour the vinaigrette over the sweet potato mixture and toss gently to coat. Garnish with fresh sage leaves. Great with chicken and pork. For a crisper texture, do not peel the potatoes. Toast the sesame seeds for a more intense flavor.

VEGETABLES & SIDES

Sweet Potato Fries

2 large sweet potatoes, peeled
3 tablespoons orange juice
1 tablespoon vegetable oil
1/2 teaspoon ground ginger
1/4 teaspoon salt
1/8 teaspoon ground red pepper

Preheat the oven to 450 degrees. Cut the sweet potatoes into 1/4- to 1/2-inch strips. Combine the orange juice, oil, ginger, salt and red pepper in a saucepan and mix well. Bring to a boil and boil for 2 minutes or until of a syrupy consistency, stirring occasionally. Remove from the heat and add the sweet potato strips, tossing to coat.

Arrange the strips in a single layer on a baking sheet coated with nonstick cooking spray. Bake for 25 minutes or until brown, turning after 10 to 15 minutes.

Chile Cheese Tomatoes

YIELD: 6 TO 8 SERVINGS

3 large or 4 medium firm tomatoes
1 cup sour cream
1 tablespoon all-purpose flour
1 teaspoon sugar
1/2 teaspoon salt
1/4 teaspoon pepper
2 tablespoons finely chopped
    green onions
2 tablespoons chopped green chiles
1 cup (4 ounces) shredded sharp
    Cheddar cheese
1/2 cup (2 ounces) shredded
    Monterey Jack cheese

Cut the tomatoes into halves and scoop out the pulp. Drain the shells upside down on paper towels for 10 minutes. Mix the sour cream, flour, sugar, salt and pepper in a bowl and stir in the green onions and green chiles. Toss the Cheddar cheese and Monterey Jack cheese together in a bowl.

Preheat the broiler. Arrange the tomato shells cut side up on a baking sheet. Mound the sour cream mixture evenly in the tomato shells and broil 4 inches from the heat source for 3 to 5 minutes or until bubbly. Sprinkle evenly with the cheese mixture and broil for 2 to 3 minutes longer or until golden brown.

COMPLIMENTS OF

Sweet-and-Sour Tomatoes and Peppers

YIELD: 8 SERVINGS

4 ripe tomatoes, cut into eighths
1/4 cup peanut oil or canola oil
4 green bell peppers, cut into
    1-inch cubes
1/2 cup white vinegar
1/4 cup sugar
soy sauce to taste
1 teaspoon cornstarch
2 tablespoons water

Place the tomatoes in a serving bowl and chill, covered, in the refrigerator. Heat a large heavy skillet until very hot and add the peanut oil. Heat until smoking and add the bell peppers.

Cook until the bell peppers are covered with gray spots, stirring constantly. Add a mixture of the vinegar and sugar and cook until bubbly, stirring frequently. Season to taste with soy sauce.

Dissolve the cornstarch in the water in a small bowl and stir into the bell pepper mixture. Cook until thickened, stirring constantly. Pour the bell pepper mixture over the chilled tomatoes and toss to mix. Serve immediately.

Green Tomato and Vidalia Onion Gratin

YIELD: 4 TO 6 SERVINGS

4 green tomatoes, sliced
4 Vidalia onions, sliced
salt and pepper to taste
2 cups (8 ounces) shredded sharp
    Cheddar cheese

Preheat the oven to 350 degrees. Layer the green tomatoes, onions, salt and pepper in a buttered 8×8-inch baking dish. Sprinkle with the cheese and bake for 30 minutes or until the cheese is bubbly.

Grilled Marinated Vegetables

YIELD: 6 SERVINGS

ELEGANT SPINACH

Bake two 12-ounce packages

frozen spinach soufflé using

the package directions. Heat

4 to 6 canned artichoke

bottoms in a saucepan and

arrange on a baking sheet.

Top each artichoke bottom

with a scoop of the warm

soufflé. Drizzle with 1 to

2 cups of hot Hollandaise

Sauce (page 177) and sprinkle

with cayenne pepper. Bake at

350 degrees for 10 minutes or

just until heated through.

Serve immediately.

1^1/2 pounds new potatoes, cut
    into halves
2 cups sliced yellow squash
2 cups sliced zucchini
12 green onions, trimmed
2 large red, yellow or orange
    bell peppers, cut into
    ^{1}/2-inch strips
^{2}/3 cup rice wine vinegar
3 tablespoons olive oil or dark
    sesame oil
2 tablespoons fresh lemon juice
2 tablespoons Dijon mustard
4 garlic cloves, minced
^{1}/2 teaspoon salt
^{1}/2 teaspoon pepper

Combine the potatoes with enough cold water to cover in a saucepan and bring to a boil. Reduce the heat and simmer for 10 minutes or until the potatoes are fork-tender; drain. Place the potatoes, squash, zucchini, green onions and bell peppers in a large sealable plastic bag.

Whisk the vinegar, olive oil, lemon juice, Dijon mustard, garlic, salt and pepper in a bowl and pour over the vegetable mixture. Seal the bag tightly and turn to coat. Marinate for 2 hours, turning occasionally.

Preheat the grill. Drain the vegetables, reserving the marinade. Arrange the vegetables in a grill basket sprayed with nonstick cooking spray. Brush the vegetables with the reserved marinade and grill over hot coals for 7^1/2 minutes. Turn the basket and baste the vegetables with the reserved marinade. Grill for 7^1/2 minutes longer.

Vegetable Tian

A flavorful vegetarian dish, such as Vegetable Tian, served with Frosty Grape Salad (page 33) and Pita Cheese Crisps (page 28) satisfies the appetite.

YIELD: 8 TO 10 SERVINGS

6 potatoes, sliced
  (about 2¹/₂ pounds)
salt to taste
4 leeks (white and green
  portions), sliced
1 tablespoon olive oil
freshly ground pepper to taste
1 tablespoon olive oil
1 pound fresh mushrooms,
  sliced
3 garlic cloves, minced
¹/₄ cup minced fresh parsley

1 tablespoon olive oil
3 red and/or yellow bell
  peppers, cut into strips
¹/₄ cup minced fresh basil
6 zucchini, sliced
1 tablespoon olive oil
¹/₂ cup milk or half-and-half
  (optional)
2 eggs, beaten (optional)
1 cup (4 ounces) freshly grated
  Parmesan cheese (optional)
fresh herbs or fresh tomato sauce

Preheat the oven to 350 degrees. Parboil the potatoes in salted water in a saucepan for 7 to 8 minutes; drain. Layer the potatoes in a lightly oiled 3-quart baking dish. Sauté the leeks in 1 tablespoon olive oil in a skillet until tender. Season to taste with salt and pepper and spoon over the potato layer, reserving the pan drippings.

Heat 1 tablespoon olive oil with the reserved pan drippings and add the mushrooms and garlic. Sauté until the mushrooms are tender and season to taste with salt and pepper. Stir in the parsley and spoon the mushroom mixture over the prepared layers, reserving the pan drippings.

Heat 1 tablespoon olive oil with the reserved pan drippings and add the bell peppers. Sauté for 2 to 3 minutes and spoon the bell peppers over the prepared layers. Sprinkle with the basil and top with the zucchini, overlapping the slices. Drizzle with 1 tablespoon olive oil and sprinkle with salt and pepper.

Whisk the milk and eggs in a bowl until blended and pour over the prepared layers. Sprinkle with the cheese and bake on the center oven rack until the potatoes are tender and the mixture is set, if using the egg mixture. Cool on a wire rack for 10 minutes. Serve garnished with fresh herbs or fresh tomato sauce.

175

Roasted Shallots

2 pounds shallots, peeled
olive oil
1 teaspoon thyme or rosemary
kosher salt to taste
freshly ground pepper to taste

Preheat the oven to 400 degrees. Toss the shallots with olive oil in a bowl and arrange in a baking pan. Sprinkle with the thyme and season to taste with salt and pepper.

Roast for 30 to 35 minutes or until golden brown, turning halfway through the roasting process. Spoon the roasted shallots around roast beef or any entrée on a platter. Substitute carrots, onions, parsnips and/or your favorite root vegetable for the shallots.

Root vegetables, such as Irish potatoes, beets, onions, or carrots, should always begin cooking in cold water. If started in boiling water, the outside cooks but it takes much longer to cook through the vegetable. Vegetables that grow below the ground should be cooked covered; those grown above the ground should be cooked uncovered.

COMPLIMENTS OF

Hollandaise Sauce

YIELD: 1 CUP

3 egg yolks
2 tablespoons fresh lemon juice
$1/8$ teaspoon prepared mustard
$1/8$ teaspoon cayenne pepper
$1/2$ cup (1 stick) butter

Process the egg yolks in a food processor
until pale yellow. Add the lemon juice,
prepared mustard and cayenne pepper and
process until combined.

Heat the butter in a saucepan to just below
the boiling point; do not allow to boil.
Gradually add the butter to the egg mixture,
processing constantly until incorporated.
If you are concerned about using raw egg
yolks, use yolks from eggs pasteurized in
their shells, which are sold at some specialty
food stores, or use an equivalent amount of
pasteurized egg substitute.

Truffle Mayonnaise

YIELD: 1 CUP

1 cup mayonnaise
$1^1/2$ teaspoons truffle oil
salt and pepper to taste

Combine the mayonnaise and truffle oil in
a bowl and mix well. Season to taste with
salt and pepper.

Store, covered, in the refrigerator. Serve as
an accompaniment to chilled asparagus.

$\mathcal{J}$ust
$\mathcal{D}$esserts

Almond Tuile with
Lemon Ice Cream *page 180*

Almond Tuile with Lemon Ice Cream

YIELD: 18 SERVINGS

Almond Tuile
9 egg whites
1 (16-ounce) package
   confectioners' sugar
4 eggs
3 tablespoons all-purpose flour
2 vanilla beans
8 ounces slivered almonds
   or hazelnuts, toasted
   and finely ground

Lemon Ice Cream
2 cups whipping cream
3 egg yolks
1 (14-ounce) can sweetened
   condensed milk
$1/2$ cup fresh lemon juice
1 teaspoon grated lemon zest
yellow food coloring (optional)

Lemon Curd and Assembly
1 cup sugar
$1/2$ cup (1 stick) butter
2 eggs, lightly beaten
2 egg yolks, lightly beaten
juice of 2 lemons

For the tuile, preheat the oven to 350 degrees. Whip the egg whites and gradually add the confectioners' sugar in a mixing bowl. Mix in the eggs and flour. Split the vanilla beans and scrape the seeds into the egg mixture, discarding the pods. Add the almonds and stir just until combined. Pipe or drop the batter onto a cookie sheet lined with a silicone baking sheet or onto a nonstick cookie sheet and spread thinly with the back of a spoon. Bake for 12 minutes. Shape the warm cookies over the bottom of a custard cup and let stand until cool. You may prepare up to 1 week in advance and store in an airtight container.

For the ice cream, beat the whipping cream in a mixing bowl until stiff peaks form. Chill in the refrigerator. Beat the egg yolks in a mixing bowl for 2 minutes. Stir in the condensed milk, lemon juice, lemon zest and food coloring and fold in the chilled whipped cream. Spoon the lemon mixture into a 2-quart electric ice cream maker and process for 45 minutes.

For the lemon curd, combine the sugar, butter, eggs, egg yolks and lemon juice in a double boiler and mix well. Cook until thickened, stirring constantly with a wooden spoon. Let stand until cool. Fill each tuile with the ice cream and top with the lemon curd.

Photograph for this recipe on page 178.

COMPLIMENTS OF

Crepe Batter
1 cup sifted all-purpose flour
4 eggs
2 tablespoons butter, melted and cooled
2 tablespoons sugar
1 1/2 teaspoons grated orange zest
1/4 teaspoon salt
3/4 cup water
3/4 cup milk

Hazelnut Filling and Assembly
1 cup sugar
1/2 cup (1 stick) butter
1 cup chopped hazelnuts, toasted
1/2 cup rum
2 tablespoons frozen orange juice
    concentrate
sugar to taste

For the batter, combine the flour, eggs, butter, sugar, orange zest and salt in a food processor and process until blended. Mix the water and milk in a measuring cup and gradually add to the flour mixture, processing constantly and scraping the side of the bowl once or twice until the consistency of thick cream. Chill, covered, for 2 to 10 hours. Heat a lightly greased crepe pan or nonstick skillet to medium heat. Pour 1/4 cup batter into pan and swirl to cover the bottom. Cook for 1 minute on each side or until light brown. The crepes may be prepared in advance and stored in the refrigerator or freezer between sheets of waxed paper.

For the filling, preheat the oven to 250 degrees. Beat 1 cup sugar and the butter in a mixing bowl until creamy, scraping the bowl occasionally. Add the hazelnuts, rum and orange juice concentrate and beat until incorporated.

Fill each crepe with 1 heaping tablespoon of the filling and roll tightly to enclose the filling. Arrange the crepes seam side down in a 9×13-inch baking dish, sprinkle with sugar to taste and spread with any remaining filling. Bake just until heated through.

Triple Citrus Cheesecake

YIELD: 12 SERVINGS

Graham Cracker Crust
1 cup graham cracker crumbs
1/3 cup packed light brown sugar
1/4 cup (1/2 stick) butter, melted

Citrus Cream Cheese Filling
32 ounces cream cheese, softened
1 cup sugar
2 tablespoons all-purpose flour
1 teaspoon vanilla extract
1 tablespoon fresh lemon juice
1 tablespoon fresh lime juice
1 tablespoon fresh orange juice
1 teaspoon grated lemon zest
1 teaspoon grated lime zest
1 teaspoon grated orange zest
4 eggs
fresh fruit

For the crust, preheat the oven to 325 degrees. Mix the graham cracker crumbs, brown sugar and butter in a bowl. Pat the crumb mixture over the bottom of a 9-inch springform pan and bake for 10 minutes. Maintain the oven temperature.

For the filling, beat the cream cheese, sugar, flour and vanilla in a mixing bowl at medium speed until blended, scraping the bowl occasionally. Add the lemon juice, lime juice, orange juice, lemon zest, lime zest and orange zest and beat until incorporated. Add the eggs 1 at a time, beating well at low speed after each addition.

Spoon the cream cheese filling into the prepared pan and bake for 60 to 65 minutes or until the center is almost set. Cool in the pan on a wire rack. Run a sharp knife around the edge of the pan and remove the side. Chill for 4 to 10 hours. Cut into wedges and garnish with fresh fruit.

COMPLIMENTS OF

Creamy Cheesecake

YIELD: 12 TO 16 SERVINGS

Graham Cracker Crust
1/3 (16-ounce) package graham crackers,
    broken
2 tablespoons sugar
1/2 cup (1 stick) unsalted butter, melted

Cream Cheese Filling
32 ounces cream cheese, softened
1 cup sugar
6 eggs
1 1/2 teaspoons vanilla extract

Sour Cream Topping and Assembly
2 cups sour cream
1/4 cup sugar
1/4 teaspoon vanilla extract
fresh strawberries or raspberries

For the crust, combine the graham crackers and sugar in a food processor and process until ground. Mix the butter with the crumb mixture in a bowl. Pat the crumb mixture over the bottom and 1 inch up the side of a 10-inch springform pan.

For the filling, preheat the oven to 375 degrees. Beat the cream cheese in a mixing bowl until light and fluffy, scraping the bowl occasionally. Blend in the sugar gradually. Beat in the eggs 1 at a time. Beat in the vanilla until blended. Spoon the cream cheese filling into the prepared pan and place on a baking sheet. Bake for 15 minutes and reduce the oven temperature to 325 degrees. Bake for 25 minutes. Cool on a wire rack for 10 minutes. Maintain the oven temperature.

For the topping, mix the sour cream, sugar and vanilla in a bowl. Spread the topping over the top of the cake, smoothing to the edge. Bake for 10 minutes longer. Cool in the pan on a wire rack. Chill, covered, for 6 to 10 hours. Remove the side of the pan and cut into wedges. Garnish each serving with fresh strawberries or raspberries.

Pretty Peachy

YIELD: VARIABLE SERVINGS

fresh peaches, cut into halves
pistachio ice cream
raspberry liqueur or raspberry jelly
mint leaves

Arrange 1 or 2 peach halves on each dessert plate. Top with a scoop of ice cream and drizzle with raspberry liqueur. Garnish with fresh mint and serve immediately.

When one has tasted watermelon, one knows what angels eat.

—Mark Twain

Amaretto Freeze

A really good make-ahead dessert that complements many menus and satisfies the palate.

YIELD: 6 SERVINGS

Chocolate Leaves
1 cup (6 ounces) chocolate chips
1 teaspoon water
fresh leaves, rinsed and patted dry

Amaretto Freeze
1 quart vanilla ice cream
2/3 cup amaretto
1/4 cup crème de cacao
2 tablespoons Triple Sec or brandy
mint leaves

For the leaves, heat the chocolate chips and water in a saucepan over low heat until blended, stirring frequently. Brush 1 side of each leaf with the chocolate mixture and chill until set. Peel off the green leaf and discard. Be sure to use nonpoisonous leaves.

For the freeze, process the ice cream, amaretto, crème de cacao and Triple Sec in a blender until smooth. Spoon the ice cream mixture into wine glasses or stemmed dessert goblets and freeze for 3 to 4 hours. Garnish each serving with chocolate leaves and/or fresh mint.

COMPLIMENTS OF

Fruit Mélange

YIELD: 4 TO 6 SERVINGS

1/4 cup Grand Marnier
1/4 cup sugar
2 pints fresh blueberries
8 ounces large Bing cherries, cut
    into halves
4 large peaches, sliced
1 pint fresh raspberries
vanilla yogurt (optional)

Mix the liqueur and sugar in a bowl. Add the blueberries, Bing cherries and peaches and toss to coat.

Spoon the blueberry mixture into Champagne glasses or stemmed dessert goblets and sprinkle with the raspberries. Serve with yogurt and your favorite cookies.

Fresh Fruit with Spiced Cream

YIELD: 4 TO 6 SERVINGS

1 cup sour cream
1 tablespoon sugar
1/2 teaspoon pumpkin pie spice
1/4 teaspoon vanilla extract
4 ripe peaches, peeled and sliced
1/2 pint fresh blueberries
1/2 pint fresh strawberries,
    cut into halves
sprigs of mint

Combine the sour cream, sugar, pumpkin pie spice and vanilla in a bowl and mix well. Chill, covered, in the refrigerator. Toss the peaches, blueberries and strawberries together in a bowl.

Spoon equal portions of the fruit mixture into 4 to 6 dessert bowls or stemmed goblets. Top each serving with a dollop of the sour cream mixture and garnish with sprigs of mint. The sour cream mixture also makes a great dip for fresh fruit.

JUST DESSERTS

YIELD: 8 SERVINGS

Lime Torte

3 cups blanched slivered
   almonds, toasted
1/2 cup sugar
5 tablespoons butter, melted
1/4 teaspoon ground cinnamon
1/3 cup black raspberry
   preserves
3 pints lime sherbet or any
   citrus sherbet or sorbet,
   slightly softened

Berry Sauce and Assembly

1/2 cup sugar
1/2 cup water
1 vanilla bean
1/2 cup sugar
31/2 pounds unsweetened
   berries or a mixture of
   unsweetened berries
strawberry fans or sprigs
   of mint

For the torte, combine the almonds and sugar in a food processor and process until finely chopped. Pour into a bowl. Mix the butter and cinnamon in a bowl and stir into the almond mixture. Using plastic wrap, pat the almond mixture over the bottom and 2 inches up the side of a 9-inch springform pan. Freeze for 15 minutes. Preheat the oven to 350 degrees and place the pan on a baking sheet. Bake for 20 minutes. Remove to a wire rack to cool.

Heat the preserves in a saucepan until melted. Spread the preserves over the baked layer. Let stand until cool and top with the sherbet. Freeze, covered with foil, until firm. You may use any flavor preserves, making sure that the chosen preserves complements the flavor of the desired sherbet.

For the sauce, mix 1/2 cup sugar and the water in a heavy saucepan. Split the vanilla bean lengthwise. Scrape the vanilla seeds into the sugar mixture and add the pod. Simmer for 5 minutes, stirring occasionally. Stir in 1/2 cup sugar and cook until the sugar dissolves, stirring frequently. Add the berries and bring to a simmer. Remove from the heat and let stand until cool. Store, covered, in the refrigerator until chilled. Discard the vanilla pod. Spoon 2 to 3 tablespoons of the sauce onto each dessert plate and top each with a slice of the torte. Garnish with strawberry fans and/or sprigs of mint.

COMPLIMENTS OF

Frozen Strawberry Meringue Torte

YIELD: 8 TO 10 SERVINGS

Nutty Graham Cracker Crust

1 cup graham cracker crumbs

3 tablespoons sugar

1/4 cup (1/2 stick) butter or
    margarine, melted

1/2 cup chopped pecans

Strawberry Filling and Assembly

2 cups sliced fresh strawberries
    (about 3 cups whole
    strawberries)

1 cup sugar

2 egg whites

1 tablespoon lemon juice

1 teaspoon vanilla extract

1/8 teaspoon salt

1/2 cup whipping cream

7 fresh strawberries,
    cut into halves

sliced fresh strawberries

For the crust, preheat the oven to 325 degrees. Combine the graham cracker crumbs, sugar and butter in a bowl and mix well. Stir in the pecans. Pat the crumb mixture over the bottom of a 10-inch springform pan and bake for 10 minutes. Cool on a wire rack.

For the filling, combine 2 cups sliced strawberries, the sugar, egg whites, lemon juice, vanilla and salt in a mixing bowl and beat at low speed just until blended. Beat at high speed for 15 minutes or until firm peaks form.

Beat the whipping cream in a mixing bowl until soft peaks form. Fold the strawberry mixture into the whipped cream and spoon into the prepared pan. Freeze, covered, for 12 hours or until firm. Remove the side of the pan and arrange the strawberry halves around the edge of the torte. Cut into wedges and top with additional sliced strawberries. If you are concerned about using raw eggs, use eggs pasteurized in their shells, which are sold at some specialty food stores, or use an equivalent amount of pasteurized egg substitute.

JUST DESSERTS

Frozen Mint Chocolate Cupcakes

YIELD: 2 DOZEN CUPCAKES

$1/2$ cup vanilla wafer crumbs
2 cups sifted confectioners' sugar
1 cup (2 sticks) butter, softened
4 ounces unsweetened chocolate, melted
4 eggs
2 teaspoons vanilla extract
$3/4$ teaspoon (or more) peppermint flavoring
$1/2$ cup vanilla wafer crumbs

Line 24 muffin cups with paper liners. Sprinkle $1/2$ cup vanilla wafer crumbs in the muffin cups. Beat the confectioners' sugar and butter in a mixing bowl until light and fluffy, scraping the bowl occasionally. Add the chocolate gradually, beating constantly until blended. Add the eggs 1 at a time, beating well after each addition. Beat in the flavorings.

Spoon the chocolate mixture evenly into the prepared muffin cups and sprinkle with $1/2$ cup vanilla wafer crumbs. Freeze until firm. Serve frozen or thawed but chilled. If you are concerned about using raw eggs, use eggs pasteurized in their shells, which are sold at some specialty food stores, or use an equivalent amount of pasteurized egg substitute.

COMPLIMENTS OF

Dutch Chocolate-Cherry Ice Cream

YIELD: 1 QUART

1 cup (heaping) pitted sweet cherries
1/4 cup cherry syrup
1 1/2 teaspoons vanilla extract
3/4 cup sugar
1/3 cup unsweetened baking cocoa
1 1/2 cups half-and-half
1 egg, lightly beaten
3/4 cup heavy cream

Combine the cherries, syrup and vanilla in a blender and process until puréed. Combine the sugar and baking cocoa in a saucepan and mix well. Stir in the half-and-half and bring to a simmer over low heat, stirring constantly. Remove from the heat.

Gradually beat the hot chocolate mixture into the egg in a bowl. Strain the chocolate mixture through a sieve into a bowl and stir in the cherry purée and heavy cream. Store, covered, in the refrigerator for 8 to 10 hours or until chilled.

Pour the chilled custard into an ice cream freezer container and freeze using the manufacturer's directions. Garnish each serving with a dollop of whipped cream, your favorite cookies and/or mint leaves. If you are concerned about using raw eggs, use eggs pasteurized in their shells, which are sold at some specialty food stores, or use an equivalent amount of pasteurized egg substitute.

Peppermint Ice Cream with Hot Fudge Sauce

YIELD: 10 SERVINGS

CHOCOLATE TRUFFLE SAUCE

Heat 1 cup heavy cream and 2 tablespoons butter in a saucepan; do not boil. Remove from the heat and stir in 2 cups semisweet chocolate chips and 1 cup milk chocolate chips. Let stand for several minutes to allow the chocolate chips to soften and then stir until blended. Store, covered, in the refrigerator. Serve over ice cream, pound cake or any dessert that needs a touch of chocolate.

Peppermint Ice Cream
8 ounces soft peppermint sticks,
    finely crushed
2 cups whole milk or 2% milk
1 cup half-and-half
1 cup heavy cream

Hot Fudge Sauce and Assembly
2 cups (12 ounces) semisweet
    chocolate chips
1 cup (6 ounces) milk
    chocolate chips
2 to 4 tablespoons heavy cream
mint leaves

For the ice cream, soak the candy in the milk in a bowl in the refrigerator for 8 to 10 hours. Pour the candy mixture into a saucepan and bring to a simmer. Remove from the heat and let stand until cool. Stir in the half-and-half and heavy cream.

Pour the cream mixture into an ice cream freezer container and freeze using the manufacturer's directions. You may substitute 2 cups half-and-half for 1 cup half-and-half and 1 cup heavy cream. Double the recipe for a large crowd.

For the sauce, combine the chocolate chips and heavy cream in a saucepan. Simmer until blended, stirring frequently. Scoop the ice cream into dessert bowls and drizzle with the warm sauce. Garnish with mint leaves.

COMPLIMENTS OF

Fruit Sherbet

YIELD: 12 SERVINGS

3 (10-ounce) packages frozen
    unsweetened raspberries,
    peaches or other fruit
3 cups buttermilk
3 cups sugar
mint leaves

Process the raspberries, buttermilk and
sugar in a blender until puréed. Pour the
raspberry mixture into an ice cream freezer
container and freeze using the manufacturer's
directions. Scoop into dessert bowls and
garnish with mint leaves and your favorite
cookies. For a real treat, use a mixture of
blueberries, blackberries and raspberries.

Boiled Custard

YIELD: 1 QUART

1 cup sugar
4 eggs
1 quart milk or half-and-half
1/2 teaspoon salt
1 teaspoon vanilla extract,
    rum or brandy
1 cup whipping cream, whipped
freshly grated nutmeg

Whisk the sugar and eggs in a heatproof
bowl until blended. Scald the milk in a
double boiler. Gradually add the hot milk
to the sugar mixture, whisking constantly.

Return the milk mixture to the double boiler
and stir in the salt. Cook over simmering
water until the mixture coats the back of a
spoon, stirring constantly. Remove from the
heat and let stand until cool. Stir in the
vanilla and whisk in the whipped cream.
Chill, covered, until serving time.

Spoon the custard into dessert goblets and
sprinkle with freshly grated nutmeg, or
spoon over pound cake on dessert plates.

Chocolate Budini with Caramel Sauce

YIELD: 6 SERVINGS

Caramel Sauce

2 cups sugar	3/4 cup heavy cream
1 cup water	1 tablespoon orange liqueur

Chocolate Budini and Assembly

6 ounces bittersweet chocolate, finely chopped	1 teaspoon vanilla extract
1 1/2 cups (3 sticks) unsalted butter, sliced	3 egg whites
	1/8 teaspoon cream of tartar
6 tablespoons sugar	6 tablespoons sugar
1/8 teaspoon salt	1 pint coffee ice cream or vanilla ice cream
3 egg yolks, at room temperature, lightly beaten	1/2 cup blanched almonds, toasted and coarsely chopped

For the sauce, bring the sugar and water to a boil in a saucepan over high heat. Reduce the heat to medium and simmer for 6 to 8 minutes or until the mixture turns an amber color. Stir in the heavy cream and remove from the heat. Mix in the liqueur. Cool slightly.

For the budini, position the oven rack in the lower 1/3 of the oven and preheat the oven to 375 degrees. Combine the chocolate, butter, 6 tablespoons sugar and the salt in a stainless steel bowl and place the bowl over hot but not simmering water. Cook until blended, stirring frequently. Remove from the heat and cool slightly. Whisk in the egg yolks and vanilla. Beat the egg whites and cream of tartar in a mixing bowl until soft peaks form. Add 6 tablespoons sugar gradually, beating constantly until stiff glossy peaks form. Fold 1/4 of the meringue into the chocolate mixture. Fold the chocolate mixture into the meringue just until combined.

Spoon the chocolate mixture evenly into 6 heatproof ramekins. You may prepare to this point up to 2 days in advance and store, loosely covered, in the refrigerator. Bring to room temperature before baking. Bake for 20 to 25 minutes or until puffed with crusty, deeply cracked tops. Top each serving with a scoop of ice cream. Sprinkle with the almonds and drizzle with the sauce.

COMPLIMENTS OF

Chocolate Cobbler

YIELD: 8 TO 10 SERVINGS

1/2 cup (1 stick) butter, melted
2 cups all-purpose flour
1 1/2 cups sugar
1/4 cup baking cocoa
1 cup milk
2 teaspoons vanilla extract
1 cup chopped pecans, toasted (optional)
2 cups sugar
1/4 cup baking cocoa
2 cups hot water

Preheat the oven to 350 degrees. Pour the butter into a 9×13-inch baking pan, tilting the pan to ensure even coverage. Mix the flour, 1 1/2 cups sugar and 1/4 cup baking cocoa in a bowl. Stir in the milk and vanilla and mix in the pecans.

Pour the chocolate batter over the butter; do not mix. Combine 2 cups sugar and 1/4 cup baking cocoa in a bowl and mix well. Sprinkle the sugar mixture evenly over the prepared layers; do not mix. Pour the hot water over the top; do not mix.

Bake for 30 to 40 minutes or until the edges pull from the sides of the pan. Serve warm topped with ice cream, whipped cream or whipped topping. You may prepare in advance and reheat in the oven or microwave.

Cooking is like love.
It should be entered into with abandon or not at all.

—*Harriet Van Horne*

Petits Pots de Crème

YIELD: 8 SERVINGS

2 cups milk
1 pound sweet chocolate, grated
8 egg yolks, lightly beaten

Scald the milk in a saucepan and stir in the chocolate. Cook until the mixture is blended and just comes to a boil, stirring constantly. Remove from the heat and let stand until cool. Add the egg yolks and stir until smooth.

Strain the chocolate mixture through a fine sieve into a bowl. Pour into 8 ramekins and chill, covered, in the refrigerator. If you are concerned about using raw egg yolks, use egg yolks from eggs pasteurized in their shells, which are sold at some specialty food stores, or use an equivalent amount of pasteurized egg substitute.

Heavenly Chocolate Fondue

YIELD: 4 CUPS

2 cups (12 ounces) semisweet
  chocolate chips
1 (14-ounce) can sweetened
  condensed milk
1 (10-ounce) jar marshmallow
  creme
1/2 cup milk
1 teaspoon vanilla extract
assorted fresh fruit chunks

Combine the chocolate chips, condensed milk, marshmallow creme, milk and vanilla in a microwave-safe bowl and mix well. Microwave on Medium for 4 to 6 minutes or until the chocolate melts. Beat until creamy. Spoon the chocolate mixture into a fondue pot or chafing dish and serve with assorted fresh fruits for dipping.

You can combine all the ingredients in a saucepan and cook over low heat until the chocolate melts, stirring constantly. Remove from the heat and beat until creamy. Serve as above.

COMPLIMENTS OF

Lamb Cake

2 cups sifted all-purpose flour	2 eggs, beaten
1 1/2 teaspoons baking powder	1 teaspoon vanilla extract
1 teaspoon baking soda	3/4 cup buttermilk
1 cup sugar	2 ounces unsweetened
1/2 cup (1 stick) butter, softened	chocolate, melted

Boiled Frosting and Assembly

2 cups sugar	1 teaspoon vanilla extract
3/4 cup water	freshly shredded coconut
1 teaspoon light corn syrup	2 jelly beans
1/8 teaspoon salt	1 chocolate chip
2 egg whites	freshly shredded coconut,
1/4 teaspoon cream of tartar	tinted green

For the cake, sift the flour, baking powder and baking soda together. Beat the sugar, butter, eggs and vanilla in a mixing bowl until light and fluffy. Add the flour mixture alternately with the buttermilk, mixing well after each addition. Add the chocolate and beat for 2 minutes. Prepare the lamb mold using the manufacturer's directions and fill with the batter. Bake as directed by the manufacturer. Cool on a wire rack for 10 minutes and invert onto a serving platter.

For the frosting, mix the sugar, water, corn syrup and salt in a saucepan. Cook over low heat until the sugar dissolves, stirring constantly. Cook, covered, for 2 to 3 minutes longer to dissolve the sugar crystals on the side of the pan. Remove the cover and cook to 240 degrees on a candy thermometer, soft-ball stage. Beat the egg whites and cream of tartar in a heatproof mixing bowl until stiff peaks form. Gradually add the hot syrup to the egg whites, beating constantly. Add the vanilla and beat for 6 minutes or until a spreading consistency. If the frosting is too thin, let stand for 3 minutes to set up slightly and then stir once or twice. Spread the frosting over the top and side of the cake. Pat the freshly shredded coconut over the surface of the cake. Position the jelly beans for the eyes and the chocolate chip for the nose. Arrange ribbon around the lamb's neck and attach the tinted coconut at the base of the lamb to represent grass.

Just Desserts

195

YIELD: 10 TO 12 SERVINGS

Cake
1 (2-layer) package devil's food cake mix
1 (6-ounce) package chocolate instant
    pudding mix
1/2 cup sugar
1 cup vegetable oil
3/4 cup water
1/4 cup vodka
4 eggs

Irish Cream Glaze and Assembly
3/4 cup confectioners' sugar
1/4 cup Irish cream

For the cake, lower the center oven rack 1 notch and preheat the oven to 350 degrees. Combine the cake mix, pudding mix and sugar in a mixing bowl and mix well. Mix the oil, water, vodka and eggs in a bowl. Add the vodka mixture to the dry ingredients and beat for 4 minutes, scraping the bowl occasionally.

Spoon the batter into a bundt pan sprayed with nonstick cooking spray and bake for 50 minutes or until a wooden pick inserted in the center comes out clean. Cool in the pan for 10 minutes and invert onto a cake plate.

For the glaze, mix the confectioners' sugar and liqueur in a bowl until smooth and of a glaze consistency. Pierce the surface of the warm cake several times with a long skewer and pour the warm glaze over the cake. Let stand until set.

COMPLIMENTS OF

Pineapple Carrot Cake

YIELD: 12 SERVINGS

Pineapple Carrot Cake

1 (15-ounce) can juice-pack
    crushed pineapple
3 cups all-purpose flour
2 cups sugar
2 teaspoons baking soda
2 teaspoons ground cinnamon
1 teaspoon ground cloves

1 teaspoon ground nutmeg
1 teaspoon ground allspice
1/2 teaspoon salt
3 cups grated carrots
1 1/2 cups vegetable oil
4 eggs

Cream Cheese Icing and Assembly

1 (16-ounce) package
    confectioners' sugar
8 ounces cream cheese, softened
1/2 cup (1 stick) butter, softened

2 teaspoons vanilla extract
1/2 cup chopped pecans or
    walnuts (optional)
mint leaves

For the cake, preheat the oven to 350 degrees. Drain the pineapple, reserving 2 tablespoons of the juice for the icing. Combine the flour, sugar, baking soda, cinnamon, cloves, nutmeg, allspice and salt in a mixing bowl and mix well. Add the pineapple, carrots, oil and eggs and beat until combined.

Spoon the batter into 3 nonstick or 3 greased and floured 8- or 9-inch cake pans. Bake for 40 minutes or until a wooden pick inserted in the layers comes out clean. Cool in the pans for 10 minutes. Invert onto a wire rack to cool completely.

For the icing, combine the confectioners' sugar, cream cheese, butter, vanilla and reserved 2 tablespoons pineapple juice in a mixing bowl and beat until spreading consistency, scraping the bowl occasionally. Stir in the pecans. Spread the icing between the layers and over the top and side of the cake. Garnish with mint leaves. You may use reduced-fat or nonfat cream cheese.

Baddour Center Walnut Cake

Walnut Cake

1^{1}/$_{2}$ (2-layer) packages banana
    cake mix
1 (4-ounce) package banana
    instant pudding mix
1 (4-ounce) package French
    vanilla instant pudding mix
1 cup pear nectar

^{3}/$_{4}$ cup vegetable oil
^{1}/$_{2}$ cup water
6 eggs
2 medium to large bananas,
    mashed
1 cup English walnuts, chopped

Caramel Icing

^{1}/$_{2}$ cup packed dark
    brown sugar
^{1}/$_{4}$ cup (^{1}/$_{2}$ stick) butter or
    margarine

^{1}/$_{4}$ cup (or more) milk
2 cups confectioners' sugar
1 teaspoon vanilla extract
^{1}/$_{8}$ teaspoon salt

For the cake, preheat the oven to 300 degrees. Combine the cake mix, pudding mixes, nectar, oil and water in a mixing bowl and beat at medium speed for 2 minutes, scraping the bowl occasionally. Add the eggs 1 at a time, beating well after each addition. Add the bananas and beat at high speed for 1 minute. Fold in the walnuts and spoon the batter into a greased tube pan.

Bake for 1^{1}/$_{4}$ hours or until the cake tests done. Cool in the pan for 10 minutes and invert onto a cake plate. One-half of a cake mix equals 2^{1}/$_{4}$ cups. If needed, you may substitute a mixture of one #2 jar of baby food pears and 1 jar of baby food pear juice for the pear nectar and water.

For the icing, combine the brown sugar, butter and milk in a saucepan and bring to a boil over low heat, stirring constantly. Boil for 1 minute. Remove from the heat and beat in the confectioners' sugar until smooth. Stir in the vanilla and salt, adding additional milk if needed for a thinner consistency. Spread the warm icing over the cake.

COMPLIMENTS OF

Yam Pound Cake with Orange Icing

Serve as a dessert, or omit the icing, slice the cake, and use the slices for French toast.

YIELD: 16 SERVINGS

Yam Cake

2 cups all-purpose flour	1¼ cups vegetable oil
1½ teaspoons baking soda	4 eggs
1½ teaspoons ground cinnamon	2 teaspoons vanilla extract
1 teaspoon ground nutmeg	1 (29-ounce) can yams, drained
1 teaspoon salt	and mashed
½ teaspoon ground cloves	1 cup chopped pecans
2 cups sugar	1 cup flaked coconut

Orange Icing and Assembly

¼ cup (½ stick) butter, softened	1 teaspoon (heaping) grated orange zest
3 ounces cream cheese, softened	½ teaspoon vanilla extract
½ (16-ounce) package confectioners' sugar	mint leaves
2 to 3 tablespoons orange juice	orange zest

For the cake, preheat the oven to 350 degrees. Sift the flour, baking soda, cinnamon, nutmeg, salt and cloves together. Beat the sugar and oil in a mixing bowl for 4 to 5 minutes, scraping the bowl occasionally. Add the eggs 1 at a time, beating well after each addition. Beat in the vanilla. Add the flour mixture and beat until blended. Mix in the yams, pecans and coconut.

Spoon the batter into a greased and floured 10-inch bundt pan and bake for 65 to 75 minutes or until the cake tests done. Cool in the pan for 15 minutes and invert onto a wire rack to cool completely. You may substitute 2 cups mashed cooked yams for the canned yams.

For the icing, beat the butter, cream cheese, confectioners' sugar, orange juice, 1 teaspoon orange zest and the vanilla in a mixing bowl until of a spreading consistency, scraping the bowl occasionally. Spread the icing over the top and side of the cake or simply sprinkle with confectioners' sugar. Garnish with mint leaves and additional orange zest.

CHOCOLATE GANACHE

Combine 2 cups semisweet chocolate morsels and 1/2 cup heavy cream in a microwave-safe bowl and microwave until blended. Stir in 3 tablespoons butter. This is a rich chocolate icing and is ideal for dipping strawberries or other fruits.

1³/4 cups sugar
1 cup all-purpose flour
1/8 teaspoon salt
4 ounces semisweet chocolate, chopped
1 cup (2 sticks) butter
4 eggs, at room temperature
2 cups pecan pieces (optional)
2 teaspoons vanilla extract
confectioners' sugar (optional)

Preheat the oven to 325 degrees. Mix the sugar, flour and salt in a mixing bowl. Heat the chocolate and butter in a saucepan over low heat until blended, stirring frequently. Add the chocolate mixture to the sugar mixture and mix well. Add the eggs 1 at a time, mixing just until moistened after each addition. Stir in the pecans and vanilla.

Spoon the batter into paper-lined muffin cups and bake for 20 to 25 minutes or until the cupcakes test done. Remove to a wire rack to cool. Dust lightly with confectioners' sugar.

Apricot Squares

YIELD: 4 DOZEN SQUARES

Brown Sugar Crust
1 cup all-purpose flour
1/3 cup packed brown sugar
1/2 cup (1 stick) butter, softened

Apricot Filling
8 ounces cream cheese, softened
1/2 cup sugar
2 eggs
1/4 cup milk
1/4 cup lemon juice
1 teaspoon vanilla extract
3 jars baby food junior apricots

For the crust, preheat the oven to 350 degrees. Combine the flour and brown sugar in a bowl and mix well. Add the butter and mix well. Pat over the bottom of a 9×13-inch baking pan and bake for 20 to 30 minutes or until light brown. Maintain the oven temperature.

For the filling, beat the cream cheese and sugar in a mixing bowl until creamy. Add the eggs, milk, lemon juice and vanilla and beat until combined. Spoon the cream cheese mixture over the baked layer. Stir the apricots and spread over the prepared layers; do not mix the layers. Bake for 25 to 30 minutes or until set. Cool in the pan on a wire rack and cut into squares.

"Chocolate Fix" Brownies

YIELD: 16 BROWNIES

1½ cups all-purpose flour
1¼ cups sugar
½ cup baking cocoa
1 teaspoon baking powder
½ teaspoon salt
¾ cup (1½ sticks) butter or
    margarine, melted
4 eggs, lightly beaten
1 cup (6 ounces) semisweet
    chocolate chips
½ cup (3 ounces) milk
    chocolate chips
½ cup (3 ounces) white
    chocolate chips
3 (2-ounce) Snickers candy bars,
    cut into ¼-inch pieces, or
    1 cup Snickers Brand
    Bite-Size Candies

Preheat the oven to 350 degrees. Combine the flour, sugar, baking cocoa, baking powder and salt in a bowl and mix well. Stir in the butter and eggs. Add the chocolate chips and mix well.

Spoon the batter into a greased 9×13-inch baking pan and bake for 30 minutes or until a wooden pick inserted in the center comes out clean. Immediately sprinkle with the candy bars. Cool in the pan on a wire rack and cut into bars. You may substitute Milky Way candy bars for the Snickers candy bars.

Kahlúa Brownies

YIELD: 16 (2-INCH) BROWNIES

2 cups sugar
1½ cups all-purpose flour
½ teaspoon baking powder
½ teaspoon salt
2 ounces unsweetened chocolate,
    chopped
⅔ cup butter
3 jumbo eggs, lightly beaten
¼ cup Kahlúa
½ teaspoon vanilla extract
¾ cup chopped pecans
2 tablespoons Kahlúa

Preheat the oven to 350 degrees. Sift the sugar, flour, baking powder and salt into a bowl and mix well. Heat the chocolate and butter in a microwave-safe bowl on Defrost until blended, stirring occasionally. Add the chocolate mixture, eggs, ¼ cup liqueur, the vanilla and pecans to the dry ingredients and mix well.

Spread the batter in an 8×8-inch baking pan and bake for 35 to 45 minutes or until the edges pull from the sides of the pan. Immediately brush the top of the brownies with 2 tablespoons liqueur. Cool in the pan on a wire rack and cut into squares. You may freeze for future use.

COMPLIMENTS OF

You can't eat just one!

YIELD: 4 TO 5 DOZEN

2 cups (4 sticks) butter
2 cups (scant) sugar
4 cups all-purpose flour
2 tablespoons ground cinnamon
    or nutmeg
2 egg yolks, lightly beaten
1 teaspoon vanilla extract
2 egg whites
2 cups chopped pecans
1 cup sugar
1 tablespoon ground cinnamon
    or nutmeg

Preheat the oven to 350 degrees. Beat the butter and 2 cups sugar in a mixing bowl until creamy, scraping the bowl occasionally. Add the flour, 2 tablespoons cinnamon, the egg yolks and vanilla and beat until blended. Press the dough over the bottom of a 10×15-inch baking pan sprayed lightly with nonstick cooking spray.

Lightly beat the egg whites in a mixing bowl. Brush the surface of the prepared layer with the egg whites and sprinkle with the pecans. Mix 1 cup sugar and 1 tablespoon cinnamon in a bowl and sprinkle over the top. Bake for 20 to 25 minutes or until light brown. Cut into squares while hot and cool in the pan.

JUST DESSERTS

Coconut Sour Bars

YIELD: 2 TO 3 DOZEN BARS

WHISKEY SAUCE

Heat 1/2 cup sugar and 1/4 cup butter in a saucepan until the butter melts and the sugar dissolves, stirring constantly. Stir a small amount of the hot mixture into 1 beaten egg in a heatproof bowl. Stir the egg into the hot mixture and cook until thickened, stirring frequently. Remove from the heat and let stand until cool. Stir in 1/2 cup whiskey. Drizzle over bread pudding, pound cake or French toast.

Crust
2 cups all-purpose flour
1/4 cup sugar
1/8 teaspoon salt
1/2 cup (1 stick) plus
    2 1/2 tablespoons butter
    or margarine

Coconut Filling
3 cups flaked coconut
2 cups packed light brown sugar
1 cup finely chopped almonds
    or pecans
4 eggs

Lime Glaze and Assembly
1 1/2 cups confectioners' sugar
2 tablespoons lime juice
2 teaspoons (heaping) grated
    lime zest

For the crust, preheat the oven to 350 degrees. Combine the flour, sugar and salt in a bowl and mix well. Cut in the butter until crumbly. Press the crumb mixture over the bottom of a 10×15-inch baking pan and bake for 15 minutes. Maintain the oven temperature.

For the filling, beat the coconut, brown sugar, almonds and eggs in a mixing bowl until combined and spread over the warm baked layer. Bake for 30 minutes. Run a sharp knife around the edges of the baked layer to loosen.

For the glaze, combine the confectioners' sugar, lime juice and lime zest in a bowl and stir until of a glaze consistency. Spread the glaze over the hot layers and let stand until cool. Cut into bars.

COMPLIMENTS OF

Crème de Menthe Squares

YIELD: 3 TO 4 DOZEN SQUARES

Chocolate Crumb Crust
1/2 cup (1 stick) butter
1/2 cup baking cocoa
1/2 cup sifted confectioners' sugar
1 egg, beaten
1 teaspoon vanilla extract
2 cups graham cracker crumbs

Crème de Menthe Filling
1/2 cup (1 stick) butter, melted
1/3 cup crème de menthe
3 cups sifted confectioners' sugar

Chocolate Glaze
1/4 cup (1/2 stick) butter
1 1/2 cups (9 ounces) chocolate chips

For the crust, heat the butter and baking cocoa in a saucepan until the butter melts, stirring frequently. Remove from the heat and stir in the confectioners' sugar, egg and vanilla. Mix in the cracker crumbs. Pat the crumb mixture over the bottom of a 9×13-inch dish. If you are concerned about using raw eggs, use eggs pasteurized in their shells, which are sold at some specialty food stores, or use an equivalent amount of pasteurized egg substitute.

For the filling, mix the butter and liqueur in a bowl. Add the confectioners' sugar and stir until blended. Add additional liqueur for a thinner consistency, or additional confectioners' sugar for a thicker consistency. Spread the filling over the prepared layer and chill in the refrigerator for 1 hour.

For the glaze, heat the butter and chocolate chips in a saucepan until blended, stirring frequently. Spread the glaze over the prepared layers and chill until set. Cut into squares.

Just Desserts

Lemon Crumb Squares

1$\frac{1}{2}$ cups sifted all-purpose flour
1 teaspoon baking powder
$\frac{1}{2}$ teaspoon salt
$\frac{2}{3}$ cup butter
1 cup packed dark brown sugar
1 cup rolled oats
1 (14-ounce) can sweetened
   condensed milk
$\frac{1}{2}$ cup lemon juice
1 teaspoon grated lemon zest

Preheat the oven to 350 degrees. Sift the flour, baking powder and salt together. Beat the butter in a mixing bowl until creamy. Add the brown sugar to the creamed butter and beat until blended. Stir in the oats and flour mixture until crumbly. Combine the condensed milk, lemon juice and lemon zest in a bowl and mix well.

Pat $\frac{1}{2}$ of the crumb mixture over the bottom of a buttered 8×12-inch baking pan. Spread the lemon mixture over the prepared layer and top with the remaining crumb mixture.

Bake for 25 minutes or until brown around the edges. Cool in the pan on a wire rack for 15 minutes and cut into small squares. Chill until firm. The flavor of the squares is enhanced if served chilled.

COMPLIMENTS OF

1¹/₂ cups sifted all-purpose flour
¹/₂ teaspoon salt
¹/₂ teaspoon ground cinnamon
¹/₄ teaspoon baking soda
³/₄ cup sugar
¹/₄ cup (¹/₂ stick) butter
2 eggs
1³/₄ cups mincemeat
1 cup chopped nuts
2 cups confectioners' sugar
lemon juice or orange juice

Preheat the oven to 350 degrees. Sift the flour, salt, cinnamon and baking soda together. Combine the sugar, butter and eggs in a mixing bowl and beat until creamy, scraping the bowl occasionally. Add the mincemeat and nuts and mix well. Stir in the flour mixture.

Spread the mincemeat mixture in a greased 9×13-inch baking pan and bake for 25 to 30 minutes or until the edges pull from the sides of the pan. Mix the confectioners' sugar with just enough lemon juice to moisten in a bowl and spread over the warm baked layer. Cool in the pan on a wire rack and cut into bars.

Just Desserts

YIELD: 3 TO 4 DOZEN BARS

Crust
2 cups all-purpose flour
1/2 cup confectioners' sugar
1 cup (2 sticks) butter, chilled

Pecan Filling
1 (14-ounce) can sweetened condensed milk
1 egg
1 teaspoon vanilla extract
1 cup (6 ounces) almond brickle chips
1 cup chopped pecans

For the crust, preheat the oven to 350 degrees. Combine the flour and confectioners' sugar in a bowl and mix well. Cut in the butter until crumbly. Pat the crumb mixture over the bottom of a 9×13-inch baking pan and bake for 15 minutes. Maintain the oven temperature. If using a glass baking dish, reduce the oven temperature to 325 degrees.

For the filling, beat the condensed milk, egg and vanilla in a mixing bowl until blended. Stir in the brickle chips and pecans. Spread the pecan mixture over the baked layer and bake for 25 minutes. Cool in the pan on a wire rack for 10 minutes. Chill, covered, in the refrigerator. Cut into bars.

COMPLIMENTS OF

Double Chocolate Cookies

YIELD: 4 DOZEN COOKIES

1 (2-layer) package Swiss chocolate
   cake mix
1/2 cup vegetable oil
2 eggs, lightly beaten
1 cup (6 ounces) semisweet
   chocolate chips or chunks
1 cup pecans, broken into
   large pieces
confectioners' sugar

Preheat the oven to 350 degrees. Combine the cake mix, oil and eggs in a mixing bowl and beat until blended. Stir in the chocolate chips and pecans.

Drop by tablespoonfuls 2 inches apart onto an ungreased cookie sheet. Bake for 8 to 9 minutes or until crisp around the edge. The cookies will not appear to be done. Cool on the cookie sheet for 2 minutes and remove to a wire rack to cool completely. Dust lightly with confectioners' sugar and store in an airtight container or freeze in sealable plastic bags for future use.

Coconut Macaroons

YIELD: 2 DOZEN COOKIES

2 1/3 cups sweetened flaked coconut
2/3 cup sugar
1/4 cup all-purpose flour
1/4 teaspoon salt
4 egg whites
1/2 teaspoon clear vanilla extract
1/2 teaspoon almond extract

Preheat the oven to 325 degrees. Line a cookie sheet with baking parchment or lightly grease. Mix the coconut, sugar, flour and salt in a bowl. Add the egg whites and flavorings and mix well. Drop by teaspoonfuls onto the prepared cookie sheet.

Bake for 18 to 20 minutes or until light brown. Cool on the cookie sheet for 2 minutes and remove to a wire rack to cool completely. Store in an airtight container.

YIELD: 3 DOZEN COOKIES

2^1/$_4$ cups all-purpose flour
^{1}/$_2$ teaspoon ground cinnamon
^{1}/$_2$ teaspoon baking powder
^{1}/$_4$ teaspoon salt
^{1}/$_4$ teaspoon baking soda
1^1/$_3$ cups sugar
^{1}/$_2$ cup (1 stick) butter
^{1}/$_4$ cup buttermilk
^{1}/$_4$ cup white corn syrup
3 eggs
^{1}/$_4$ cup brewed tea
^{1}/$_4$ cup preserves (peach, apricot or pineapple)
1^1/$_2$ pounds pecans, chopped
12 ounces dates, chopped
12 ounces candied pineapple, chopped
12 ounces candied cherries
8 ounces raisins

Combine the flour, cinnamon, baking powder, salt and baking soda in a bowl and mix well. Beat the sugar, butter, buttermilk, corn syrup, eggs, tea and preserves in a mixing bowl until combined. Add the flour mixture and mix well. Chill, covered, for 8 to 10 hours.

Preheat the oven to 275 to 300 degrees. Stir the pecans, dates, pineapple, cherries and raisins into the chilled dough. Drop by teaspoonfuls 2 inches apart onto a cookie sheet and bake for 15 minutes. Cool on the cookie sheet for 2 minutes and remove to a wire rack to cool completely. Store in an airtight container.

COMPLIMENTS OF

Spicy Ginger Cookies

YIELD: 4 TO 5 DOZEN COOKIES

2 cups all-purpose flour
2 teaspoons baking soda
1 cup sugar
3/4 cup shortening
1/4 cup molasses
1 egg
1 teaspoon ground cinnamon
1 teaspoon ground cloves
3/4 teaspoon ground ginger
1/2 teaspoon mace
1/2 teaspoon ground allspice
1/4 teaspoon salt

Preheat the oven to 375 degrees. Mix the flour and baking soda together. Beat the sugar, shortening, molasses and egg in a mixing bowl until creamy, scraping the bowl occasionally. Add the cinnamon, cloves, ginger, mace, allspice and salt and mix well. Add the flour mixture 1/2 cup at a time, beating well after each addition.

Drop by teaspoonfuls 2 inches apart onto a cookie sheet. Bake for 8 to 10 minutes or to the desired crispness. Cool on the cookie sheet for 2 minutes and remove to a wire rack to cool completely. Store in an airtight container.

CHAMBORD
BERRY SAUCE

Thaw and drain one

10-ounce package frozen

strawberries, reserving the

juice. Mix the reserved

juice, 1/3 cup Chambord,

1 tablespoon lemon juice

and 1 tablespoon cornstarch

in a saucepan and cook over

low heat until the consistency

of a light syrup, stirring

frequently. Remove from the

heat and let stand until cool.

Stir in 1/3 cup Chambord,

1 pint blackberries and the

strawberries. Chill, covered,

in the refrigerator. Serve over

pound cake, angel food cake

or vanilla ice cream. Garnish

with sprigs of mint.

1 cup sugar
1 tablespoon all-purpose flour
1 teaspoon baking powder
1/2 cup (1 stick) butter
11/2 cups quick-cooking oats
1 egg, lightly beaten
1 teaspoon vanilla extract

Preheat the oven to 350 degrees. Line a 14×17-inch cookie sheet with foil dull side up. Sift the sugar, flour and baking powder into a bowl and mix well. Heat the butter in a saucepan over low heat until melted. Stir in the oats and sugar mixture. Mix in the egg and stir in the vanilla. Remove from the heat.

Drop by 1/2 teaspoonfuls 2 inches apart onto the prepared cookie sheet. Bake for 8 to 9 minutes or until bubbles no longer appear and the cookies are light brown. Remove the foil with the cookies to a hard surface and let stand until cool. Peel the cookies from the foil and store in an airtight container or freeze for future use.

Crisp Oat Cookies

YIELD: 5 DOZEN COOKIES

1³/4 cups all-purpose flour
¹/2 teaspoon baking soda
¹/4 teaspoon salt
¹/2 cup (1 stick) butter, softened
¹/2 cup granulated sugar
¹/2 cup packed brown sugar
1 egg white, beaten
¹/2 cup vegetable oil
¹/4 teaspoon vanilla extract
¹/2 cup quick-cooking oats
¹/2 cup cornflakes
¹/4 cup pecans, finely chopped
¹/4 cup flaked coconut

Preheat the oven to 325 degrees. Mix the flour, baking soda and salt together. Beat the butter in a mixing bowl until creamy. Add the granulated sugar and brown sugar gradually, beating constantly at medium speed until blended. Stir in the egg white and beat in the oil and vanilla until combined. Add the flour mixture and beat until blended. Stir in the oats, cornflakes, pecans and coconut.

Shape the dough into ¹/2-inch balls and arrange 2 inches apart on an ungreased cookie sheet. Flatten with a fork and bake for 15 minutes. Cool on the cookie sheet for 2 minutes and remove to a wire rack to cool completely. Store in an airtight container.

The Best Sugar Cookies

YIELD: 3 DOZEN COOKIES

3 cups all-purpose flour
1 teaspoon baking powder
¹/4 teaspoon salt
1 cup sugar
1 cup (2 sticks) butter
1 egg
1 teaspoon vanilla extract

Preheat the oven to 400 degrees. Mix the flour, baking powder and salt together. Combine the sugar, butter, egg and vanilla in a mixing bowl and beat at medium speed until light and fluffy, scraping the bowl occasionally. Add the flour mixture and beat at low speed until a soft dough forms.

Roll the dough ¹/8 inch thick on a lightly floured surface and cut with a 3-inch cutter dipped in flour. Arrange the cookies 2 inches apart on an ungreased cookie sheet and bake for 9 to 12 minutes or until the edges are golden brown.

Cool on the cookie sheet for 2 minutes and remove to a wire rack to cool completely. If desired, frost the cookies with confectioners' sugar icing or top with tinted sprinkles. Store in an airtight container or freeze for future use.

JUST DESSERTS

Graham Cracker Crust

1 cup graham cracker crumbs   1/4 cup (1/2 stick) butter, melted
1/4 cup sugar

Pie

1 1/4 cups shredded coconut   4 eggs
2 tablespoons unflavored gelatin   1/2 cup amaretto
1/3 cup cold water   1 teaspoon almond extract
1 cup sugar   3 cups whipping cream

For the crust, combine the graham cracker crumbs and sugar in a bowl and mix well. Add the butter and stir until crumbly. Pat the crumb mixture over the bottom of a 9-inch springform pan and chill in the refrigerator.

For the pie, preheat the oven to 300 degrees. Spread the coconut on a baking sheet and toast until golden brown, stirring occasionally. Remove the coconut to a plate to cool. Sprinkle the gelatin over the cold water in a small bowl and let stand for 5 minutes. Place the bowl containing the gelatin mixture in a larger bowl and add enough hot water to reach halfway up the side of the smaller bowl. Let stand until the gelatin dissolves and stir.

Beat the sugar and eggs in a mixing bowl at medium speed until fluffy. Fold in the gelatin mixture, liqueur and flavoring. Beat the whipping cream in a mixing bowl until stiff peaks form. Fold 1 cup of the toasted coconut into the whipped cream and fold the whipped cream mixture into the egg mixture. Spoon into the prepared pan and sprinkle with the remaining 1/4 cup coconut. Chill, covered, until set. If you are concerned about using raw eggs, use eggs pasteurized in their shells, which are sold at some specialty food stores, or use an equivalent amount of pasteurized egg substitute.

COMPLIMENTS OF

Chocolate Buttermilk Pie

YIELD: 6 TO 8 SERVINGS

1 refrigerator pie pastry
2 cups (12 ounces) chocolate chips
2 tablespoons butter
7 eggs, at room temperature
1½ cups sugar
1 cup buttermilk
1 teaspoon vanilla extract
⅛ teaspoon salt
whipped cream
baking cocoa or finely ground chocolate

Preheat the oven to 325 degrees. Fit the pastry into a deep-dish pie plate and trim the edge. Melt the chocolate chips and butter in a double boiler, stirring frequently. Or microwave the chocolate mixture in a microwave-safe dish, stirring every 30 seconds until smooth. Let stand until cool.

Beat the eggs, sugar, buttermilk, vanilla and salt in a mixing bowl until blended. Stir in the chocolate mixture and spoon the filling into the pastry-lined pie plate. Bake for 1 hour. Cool on a wire rack. Cut into wedges and top each serving with a dollop of whipped cream sprinkled with baking cocoa or ground chocolate.

YIELD: 8 TO 10 SERVINGS

1 (4-ounce) package vanilla pudding and
    pie filling mix
1½ tablespoons sugar
1½ tablespoons all-purpose flour
1 (12-ounce) can evaporated milk, or
    1½ cups half-and-half
1 (7-ounce) can coconut milk
1 coconut milk can water or milk
1 egg yolk
½ cup (1 stick) butter
1 (7-ounce) can flaked coconut
1 teaspoon coconut extract
1 teaspoon vanilla extract
1 baked (10-inch) deep-dish pie shell
sweetened whipped cream
toasted coconut

Combine the pudding mix, sugar and flour in a double boiler and mix well. Whisk the evaporated milk, coconut milk, water and egg yolk in a bowl until blended. Add the liquid mixture to the sugar mixture and mix well.

Cook until thickened and of a pudding consistency, stirring frequently. Remove from the heat and stir in the butter, flaked coconut and flavorings. Spoon the coconut filling into the pie shell and chill, covered with waxed paper or plastic wrap, in the refrigerator. Top with sweetened whipped cream and/or toasted coconut

Tart Shells

YIELD: 1 DOZEN TART SHELLS

2 1/2 cups all-purpose flour
1 cup (2 sticks) butter, chilled
    and cut into chunks
3 tablespoons sugar
1 teaspoon salt
1/4 cup ice water
2 egg yolks

Preheat the oven to 350 degrees. Combine the flour, butter, sugar and salt in a food processor and process until crumbly. Pour in the ice water. Add the egg yolks 1 at a time, processing constantly just until combined.

Pat the dough 1/4 inch thick on a lightly floured surface and cut into rounds. Fit the rounds into small tart pans or muffin cups. Bake filled or unfilled for 15 to 20 minutes or until light brown. Freeze unfilled shells for future use.

Cream Puffs

YIELD: 24 TO 30 PUFFS

1 cup milk
1/3 cup butter
1/4 teaspoon salt
1 cup all-purpose flour
5 eggs, at room temperature

Preheat the oven to 425 degrees. Bring the milk, butter and salt to a boil in a saucepan. Stir in the flour with a wooden spoon and cook until the dough pulls from the side of the pan. Remove from the heat and add the eggs 1 at a time, beating until smooth and glossy but not shiny after each addition.

Spoon the dough into a pastry bag and pipe twenty-four to thirty 1-inch puffs 1 1/2 inches apart onto a baking sheet sprayed with nonstick cooking spray.

Bake for 10 minutes and reduce the oven temperature to 350 degrees. Bake for 25 minutes longer or until golden brown and puffed. Remove to a wire rack to cool. Fill the cream puffs with lemon curd, ice cream, chicken salad or seafood salad.

Chefs'
Recipes

Beef Tenderloin Stuffed with
Lobster and Asparagus *page 227*

Crab Meat Almond Dip

Your Personal Chef, Nashville, Tennessee

YIELD: 4 CUPS

12 ounces cream cheese, softened
1/4 cup mayonnaise
2 tablespoons dry white wine
1 tablespoon Dijon mustard
3/4 teaspoon confectioners' sugar
1/4 teaspoon onion juice or onion powder
3 garlic cloves, crushed
8 ounces lump crab meat, drained and
    shells removed
1/4 cup almond slivers, toasted
2 tablespoons chopped fresh parsley
paprika

Preheat the oven to 350 degrees. Combine the cream cheese, mayonnaise, wine, Dijon mustard, confectioners' sugar, onion juice and garlic in a food processor and process until blended. Fold in the crab meat.

Spoon the crab meat mixture into an ovenproof chafing dish and sprinkle with the almonds, parsley and paprika. Bake until bubbly. Serve with assorted toast rounds or corn chips.

COMPLIMENTS OF

Black Bean Tart

Your Personal Chef, Nashville, Tennessee

YIELD: 6 TO 8 SERVINGS

Spicy Crumb Crust

1 1/2 cups all-purpose flour
1 teaspoon paprika
1 teaspoon ground cumin
1 teaspoon chili powder

1/2 teaspoon salt
6 tablespoons butter, chilled
4 to 6 tablespoons cold water

Black Bean Filling

2 (15-ounce) cans black beans, drained and rinsed
2 teaspoons sour cream
1/2 teaspoon salt
1 (10-ounce) package frozen corn, thawed
1 tablespoon vegetable oil
1/2 cup chopped red bell pepper

1/2 cup chopped green onions
1/3 cup minced fresh cilantro
2 tablespoons chopped green chiles
1/2 teaspoon salt
1/4 teaspoon pepper
1 1/2 cups (6 ounces) shredded Monterey Jack cheese

For the crust, preheat the oven to 350 degrees. Combine the flour, paprika, cumin, chili powder and salt in a food processor and mix well. Add the butter and pulse until crumbly. Add the cold water gradually, processing constantly until the mixture forms a ball. Pat the dough over the bottom and up the side of an ungreased tart pan with removable bottom. Line the pastry with foil and dried beans. Bake for 10 minutes and remove the beans and foil. Bake for 8 to 10 minutes longer. Maintain the oven temperature.

For the filling, process 1 cup of the beans, the sour cream and 1/2 teaspoon salt in a food processor until smooth. Spread the bean mixture over the bottom of the baked tart shell. Sauté the corn in the oil in a skillet until tender. Remove from the heat and stir in the bell pepper, green onions, cilantro, green chiles, 1/2 teaspoon salt and the pepper. Add the remaining beans and cheese and mix well.

Mound the bean mixture over the prepared layer and bake for 20 to 25 minutes. Cut into wedges and top with additional sour cream. Double the recipe and bake in a 13×18-inch baking pan. Cut into squares and serve as an hors d'oeuvre.

Oysters Harlon

The late Harlon Fields, Four Flames, Memphis, Tennessee

YIELD: 2 DOZEN OYSTERS

24 shucked fresh oysters
salt and pepper to taste
all-purpose flour for coating
1 cup steak sauce
2 tablespoons Worcestershire sauce
2 tablespoons fresh lemon juice
2 jiggers sherry or madeira
2 tablespoons all-purpose flour
3 tablespoons water

Preheat the grill. Sprinkle the oysters with salt and pepper and coat with flour. Brush the grill rack with butter and grill the oysters over hot coals until brown on both sides, or sauté lightly in a skillet. Arrange the oysters in a single layer on a baking sheet and cover to keep warm.

Preheat the broiler. Heat the steak sauce, Worcestershire sauce, lemon juice and sherry in a saucepan; do not allow to boil. Blend 2 tablespoons flour with 3 tablespoons water and add to the sauce. Cook until thickened, stirring frequently. Spoon approximately 1 tablespoon of the sauce over each oyster and broil until bubbly. Serve immediately.

COMPLIMENTS OF

Warm Poached Oysters with Fennel and Rosé Champagne Cream

Cullen Kent, La Tourelle, Memphis, Tennessee

YIELD: 8 SERVINGS

1 bottle rosé Champagne
4 cups heavy cream
2 fennel bulbs, thinly sliced
10 cherry or grape tomatoes,
    cut into halves
chopped fresh chives
olive oil to taste
salt and pepper to taste
1 quart oysters
candied orange zest

Heat the Champagne in a saucepan until reduced by $1/2$. Stir in the cream and cook until the mixture is of a sauce consistency, stirring frequently. Strain through a fine sieve into a bowl and cover to keep warm.

Toss the fennel, tomatoes and chives in a bowl with the desired amount of olive oil and season to taste with salt and pepper. Heat the undrained oysters in a saucepan until warm and cover.

Spoon equal portions of the fennel onto 8 serving plates. Arrange the warm oysters around the outer edge of the salad and cover the oysters with the Champagne cream. Garnish with candied orange zest.

Paulette's House Tarragon Vinaigrette

Paulette's, Memphis, Tennessee

YIELD: 3 CUPS

2 cups vegetable oil
1 cup tarragon vinegar
juice of $1/2$ lemon
2 tablespoons salt
2 teaspoons tarragon
1 teaspoon coarsely ground pepper
$1/4$ teaspoon dry mustard
$1/8$ teaspoon Tabasco sauce
$1/8$ teaspoon crushed garlic

Combine the oil, vinegar, lemon juice, salt, tarragon, pepper, dry mustard, Tabasco sauce and garlic in a blender and process at medium speed for 25 to 30 seconds. Store in an airtight container in the refrigerator.

Pork Tenderloin with Pinot Noir Sauce

Paulette's, Memphis, Tennessee

YIELD: VARIABLE SERVINGS

Pinot Noir Sauce
2 cups demi-glace
$3/4$ cup pinot noir
$1/4$ cup minced shallots
$3/4$ teaspoon unsalted butter

Pork Tenderloin
pork tenderloin, cut into
    1-inch slices
bacon slices

For the sauce, combine the demi-glace, wine and shallots in a heavy saucepan and bring to a simmer. Simmer for 15 minutes or until slightly thickened, stirring frequently. Whisk in the butter until blended and remove from the heat. Cover to keep warm.

For the pork, preheat the grill. Stack 2 or 3 slices of pork, wrap with a slice of bacon and secure with a wooden pick. Repeat this process with the remaining pork and remaining bacon.

Grill the pork stacks over hot coals until the sliced pork reaches the desired degree of doneness and the bacon is brown and crisp. Arrange the pork stacks in a pool of the sauce on heated serving plates.

COMPLIMENTS OF

Cool Avocado Soup with Mango Salsa

Rick Farmer, Jarrett's Restaurant, Memphis, Tennessee

YIELD: 6 SERVINGS

Mango Salsa

3 mangoes, cut into
   1/4-inch pieces
4 ripe Roma tomatoes, cut into
   1/4-inch pieces
1 poblano chile, cut into
   1/4-inch pieces
1 red bell pepper, cut into
   1/4-inch pieces
1 red onion, cut into
   1/4-inch pieces

juice of 3 limes
1 tablespoon honey
1 tablespoon grated fresh ginger
1 tablespoon chopped fresh
   cilantro
1 teaspoon chopped fresh garlic
salt and pepper to taste

Avocado Soup

3 or 4 avocados
juice of 3 lemons
juice of 4 limes

3 cups chicken stock
2 cups half-and-half
salt and pepper to taste

For the salsa, combine the mangoes, tomatoes, poblano chile, bell pepper and onion in a bowl and mix well. Stir in the lime juice, honey, ginger, cilantro and garlic. Season to taste with salt and pepper. Chill, covered, in the refrigerator.

For the soup, process the avocados, lemon juice and lime juice in a food processor until smooth. Add the stock, half-and-half, salt and pepper and process until blended. Chill, covered, in the refrigerator. Ladle the chilled soup into soup bowls and top each serving with some of the salsa.

Alex and Judd Grisanti, Elfo's, Memphis, Tennessee

YIELD: 4 TO 6 SERVINGS

$1/2$ cup (1 stick) unsalted butter
4 ribs celery, chopped
1 large onion, chopped
1 cup dry white wine
34 ounces clam juice
$1^1/2$ tablespoons Old Bay seasoning
$1/2$ to 1 teaspoon shrimp base
1 pound crawfish, cooked
2 cups half-and-half
1 cup heavy cream
salt and freshly ground pepper to taste

Heat the butter in a large saucepan over medium-low heat and add the celery and onion. Sweat the vegetables until tender. Stir in the wine and cook until reduced by $1/2$, stirring frequently. Add the clam juice, Old Bay seasoning and shrimp base and bring to a boil; reduce the heat.

Simmer for 20 minutes, stirring occasionally. Remove from the heat and stir in the crawfish. Process the crawfish mixture in a blender or food processor until puréed. Return the purée to the saucepan and stir in the half-and-half and heavy cream. Season to taste with salt and pepper. Simmer just until heated through, stirring frequently. Ladle into soup bowls and serve immediately.

COMPLIMENTS OF

Beef Tenderloin Stuffed with Lobster and Asparagus

Steve and Katherine Mistilis, C .C. E., Bridgewater House, Cordova, Tennessee

YIELD: 8 SERVINGS

Lemon Butter Sauce

$1/2$ cup (1 stick) butter, melted

2 tablespoons lemon juice

1 tablespoon chopped fresh basil

Beef Tenderloin

8 ounces (about) fresh asparagus

salt to taste

2 (4-ounce) lobster tails, fresh
   or frozen

1 (3- to 4-pound) beef
   tenderloin, trimmed

8 ounces (about) fresh crab meat,
   drained and shells removed

Red Wine Sauce and Assembly

$1/2$ cup chopped green onions

$1/4$ cup ($1/2$ stick) butter

$1/2$ cup red wine

1 tablespoon chopped fresh basil

salt and pepper to taste

For the lemon butter sauce, whisk the butter, lemon juice and basil in a bowl.

For the tenderloin, preheat the oven to 425 degrees. Discard the woody ends of the asparagus spears and blanch the spears in boiling water in a saucepan; drain. Bring enough salted water to cover the lobster tails to a boil in a saucepan. Add the lobster tails to the boiling water and return to a boil. Reduce the heat. Simmer for $2^1/2$ to 3 minutes for fresh lobster tails, or 5 to 6 minutes for frozen lobster tails; drain. Carefully remove the meat from the lobster tails and cut each portion into halves. Cut the tenderloin lengthwise into halves to within $1/2$ inch of the bottom and lay flat on a hard surface. Place the lobster meat end to end down the center of the tenderloin and arrange the asparagus and crab meat over the lobster according to the space available and drizzle with the sauce. Wrap both sides around the filling and secure at 1- to 2-inch intervals with kitchen twine. Arrange the tenderloin on a rack in a baking pan and bake for 30 to 45 minutes or until a meat thermometer registers 120 degrees for rare, or to the desired degree of doneness.

For the wine sauce, sauté the green onions in the butter in a saucepan until tender. Add the wine and cook to a sauce consistency. Stir in the basil, salt and pepper. Slice the tenderloin as desired and serve with the wine sauce.

Photograph for this recipe is on page 218.

227

Shish-Ka-Bob

Dimitri Taras, Jim's Place East, Memphis, Tennessee

YIELD: 8 SERVINGS

2 pounds beef or lamb tenderloin
$1/2$ cup burgundy
$1/2$ cup vegetable oil
3 garlic cloves, minced
2 teaspoons oregano
2 green bell peppers, cut into quarters
2 red bell peppers, cut into quarters
2 onions, cut into quarters
16 mushrooms
salt and pepper to taste
juice of 4 lemons
$1/4$ cup vegetable oil
$1/2$ teaspoon oregano

Cut the beef into 1- to $1^1/2$-inch cubes. Mix the wine, $1/2$ cup oil, the garlic and 2 teaspoons oregano in a nonreactive bowl. Add the beef to the wine mixture and toss to coat. Marinate, covered, in the refrigerator for 8 to 10 hours; drain.

Preheat the grill. Steam the bell peppers and onions for 5 minutes and drain. Thread the mushrooms, beef, bell peppers and onions alternately onto 8 skewers, beginning and ending with the mushrooms. Sprinkle with salt and pepper.

Grill over hot coals to the desired degree of doneness, turning frequently. Remove the skewers from the grill and immediately baste with a mixture of the lemon juice, $1/4$ cup oil and $1/2$ teaspoon oregano. Serve immediately with hot cooked rice or pasta.

COMPLIMENTS OF

Pan-Roasted Salmon with Ginger Crust

Three Oaks Grill, Germantown, Tennessee

YIELD: 1 SERVING

Ginger Crust

2 cups dry bread crumbs
2 tablespoon finely chopped
    fresh cilantro

1/4 cup minced fresh ginger
1/4 cup (1/2 stick) butter,
    softened

Pan-Roasted Salmon

1 (8-ounce) salmon fillet,
    skinless
1/4 teaspoon kosher salt

1/8 teaspoon freshly
    ground pepper
2 tablespoons olive oil

Soy Beurre Blanc and Assembly

2 cups (4 sticks) unsalted butter,
    softened
1 tablespoon minced fresh ginger
1/4 cup dry white wine

1/2 cup heavy cream
2 tablespoons soy sauce
black sesame seeds
1 sprig of cilantro

For the crust, mix the bread crumbs, cilantro and ginger in a bowl. Add the butter and knead until the mixture adheres. Set aside at room temperature; do not chill or store for future use.

For the salmon, preheat the oven to 350 degrees. Sprinkle both sides of the fillet with the salt and pepper. Heat an ovenproof skillet over high heat until very hot. Add the olive oil to the hot skillet and heat until almost smoking. Arrange the fillet top side down in the hot oil and sear for 1 minute or until golden brown. Turn the fillet and sear the remaining side. Remove from the heat. Press 1/4 cup of the crust over the top of the fillet until covered. Bake to the desired degree of doneness. Cover to keep warm.

For the beurre blanc, heat 1 tablespoon of the butter in a heavy saucepan. Add the ginger and cook for 10 seconds. Stir in the wine and simmer until most of the wine evaporates. Add the heavy cream and cook until thickened. Whisk in the remaining butter 1 to 2 teaspoons at a time until incorporated. Stir in the soy sauce. Line a serving plate with 1/4 cup of the beurre blanc and arrange the fillet crust side up in the center of the plate. Sprinkle sesame seeds over the sauce and arrange the cilantro sprig on the fillet.

Spicy Asian Tuna Tartare with
Avocado, Mango and Sweet Soy Glaze

Wally Joe, Wally Joe, Memphis, Tennessee

YIELD: 4 SERVINGS

2 cups soy sauce
1/2 cup sugar
1/2 cup mirin
1 pound sashimi tuna
2 tablespoons soy sauce
2 teaspoons sambal oelek
1 tablespoon chopped pickled ginger
1 1/2 teaspoons sesame oil
1 teaspoon black sesame seeds, toasted
1 ripe avocado, thinly sliced
1 ripe mango, thinly sliced
1 package daikon sprouts

Combine 2 cups soy sauce, the sugar and mirin in a saucepan and bring to a boil. Boil to a syrupy consistency, stirring occasionally.

Clean the tuna and remove all the sinew. Cut into small cubes. Mix 2 tablespoons soy sauce, the sambal oelek, ginger, sesame oil and sesame seeds in a bowl and add the tuna, tossing to coat. Taste and adjust the seasonings if desired. Chill, covered, in the refrigerator.

Fan the avocado slices and mango slices alternately in the center of a decorative dinner plate. Mound the tuna tartare over the avocado and mango slices. Drizzle the soy sauce glaze around the tuna, avocado and mango. Arrange the sprouts on top of the tuna and serve with a glass of Alsatian riesling.

Sambal, sesame oil and pickled ginger can be found in Asian markets. Daikon sprouts can be found in health food stores.

COMPLIMENTS OF

Trout Meunière

Stan Gibson, University Club, Memphis, Tennessee

YIELD: 4 SERVINGS

4 (10-ounce) semi-boneless trout fillets
milk
1 cup all-purpose flour
2 tablespoons salt
1 teaspoon white pepper
1 teaspoon paprika
1/4 cup (about) vegetable oil
1/2 cup (1 stick) butter
1/2 cup chopped fresh parsley
juice of 1 lemon

Soak the fillets in milk in a shallow dish for several minutes; drain. Mix the flour, salt, white pepper and paprika in a bowl and coat the fillets with the flour mixture. Heat the oil in a large skillet and add the fillets skin side up.

Sauté for 45 to 60 seconds per side. Remove the fillets to a heated platter, discarding the pan drippings. Immediately add the butter, parsley and lemon juice to the hot skillet and cook until the butter is light brown, stirring constantly. Drizzle the butter sauce over the fillets and serve immediately.

Pernod-Glazed Jumbo "Blue Crab Lumps" Rockefeller

Dean Pugel, Richland Country Club, Nashville, Tennessee

YIELD: 4 SERVINGS

Saffron Potato Purée

3/4 cup milk

1/16 teaspoon saffron

2 large Idaho potatoes, cooked
 and peeled

1/4 cup (1/2 stick) butter

kosher salt and cracked pepper

Pernod Spinach

2 bunches spinach, stems
 removed and spinach
 blanched

1/4 cup minced shallots

2 tablespoons butter

2 tablespoons Pernod

1 teaspoon cracked fennel seeds,
 toasted

kosher salt and cracked pepper

Mousseline Sauce and Assembly

2 eggs

juice of 1 lemon

Tabasco sauce to taste

kosher salt and cracked pepper

Worcestershire sauce to taste

3 cups clarified butter, heated

1/2 cup whipping cream, whipped

8 ounces steamed blue crab

For the potato purée, heat the milk in a saucepan and stir in the saffron. Remove from the heat and steep for several minutes. Beat the potatoes, butter, salt and pepper into the milk mixture until smooth.

For the spinach, coarsely chop the spinach. Sauté the shallots in the butter in a sauté pan until tender. Stir in the spinach, liqueur, fennel seeds, salt and pepper. Remove from the heat.

For the mousseline sauce, process the eggs, lemon juice, Tabasco sauce, salt, pepper and Worcestershire sauce in a blender until smooth. Add the warm clarified butter gradually, processing constantly until thickened. Pour into a bowl and fold in the whipped cream. Arrange 4 metal baking rings on a baking sheet and spoon 1/2 inch of the potato purée into each. Spread a 1/2-inch layer of the spinach over the top of the purée and layer each with 2 ounces of the crab meat. Top with enough mousseline sauce to cover and broil until brown.

Low Country Shrimp and Grits

Jeff Dunham, The Grove Grill, Memphis, Tennessee

YIELD: 8 SERVINGS

Speckle Heart Grits

2 cups chicken stock

2 cups milk

1/4 cup (1/2 stick) butter

1 cup stone-ground grits

1 cup chicken stock

salt to taste

Tabasco sauce to taste

Shrimp and Assembly

2 pounds (16- to 20-count)
   shrimp, peeled and deveined

4 teaspoons Cajun seasoning

1/4 cup vegetable oil

1/4 cup minced garlic

4 ounces tasso, chopped

1/2 cup dry white wine

1/4 cup chopped fresh herbs
   (parsley, thyme, rosemary
   and basil)

1 cup shrimp stock

1/4 cup (1/2 stick) butter

salt to taste

1/4 cup chopped fresh scallions

For the grits, combine 2 cups stock, the milk and butter in a double boiler and bring to a simmer, stirring occasionally. Add the grits and simmer for 5 minutes, stirring constantly. Cook for 1 to 2 hours longer, adding 1 cup stock as needed for the desired consistency and stirring occasionally. Season to taste with salt and Tabasco sauce.

For the shrimp, toss the shrimp with the Cajun seasoning in a bowl. Heat a large skillet over medium-high heat and add the oil, garlic, tasso and shrimp. Sauté for 2 to 3 minutes. Stir in the wine and herbs and cook for 1 to 2 minutes longer. Add the stock and bring to a boil.

Spoon the grits evenly into 8 bowls. Using a slotted spoon, spoon the shrimp and tasso evenly over each serving of grits. Return the skillet to the heat and simmer until the mixture is reduced by 1/2, stirring frequently. Remove from the heat and whisk in the butter. Season to taste with salt. Spoon the sauce evenly over the shrimp and grits and sprinkle with the scallions.

The Bridgewater House Eggs Benedict

Steven Mistilis, Bridgewater House, Cordova, Tennessee

YIELD: 4 SERVINGS

32 fresh spinach leaves, trimmed, rolled and sliced
12 slices Canadian bacon
8 eggs
salt and pepper to taste
paprika to taste
1/2 cup (2 ounces) yellow Cheddar cheese, shredded
1/2 cup (2 ounces) white Cheddar cheese, shredded
4 English muffins, split and toasted
1 recipe Hollandaise Sauce (page 177)
16 asparagus spears, woody ends removed and
    spears blanched
fresh fruit

Preheat the oven to 350 degrees. Spray four 4-inch ramekins with nonstick baking spray and coat with butter. Place the ramekins on a baking sheet. Arrange 8 rolled and sliced spinach leaves in each of the prepared ramekins and layer each with 3 slices of the bacon. Break 2 eggs over the top of each and sprinkle with salt, pepper and paprika. Sprinkle with the cheese.

Bake for 20 to 25 minutes or until light brown. Arrange 1 muffin on each of 4 serving plates. Separate the crusts from the sides of the ramekins with a paring knife. Carefully lift out the Benedicts and arrange on the English muffins. Drizzle with Hollandaise Sauce and dust with paprika. Arrange 4 asparagus spears at an angle over each Benedict and garnish with fresh fruit.

Grand Marnier Meringue Grapefruit

Katherine Mistilis, C. C. E., Bridgewater House, Cordova, Tennessee

YIELD: 4 SERVINGS

2 pink, white or red grapefruit
1/4 cup Grand Marnier
2 egg whites
1/16 teaspoon cream of tartar (optional)
1 tablespoon sugar
2 strawberries, cut into halves
4 mint leaves

Preheat the oven to 375 degrees. Cut the grapefruit into halves with a grapefruit knife. Cut around the rims and inside the membranes to loosen the sections. Drain the excess juice and pour the liqueur over the top. Place each grapefruit half in an ovenproof ramekin.

Beat the egg whites in a copper bowl with a balloon whisk or electric mixer until frothy, adding the cream of tartar if not using a copper bowl. Add the sugar gradually and beat until stiff peaks form.

Spoon the meringue evenly over the top of each grapefruit half, spreading to the edges. Swirl and peak the meringue using the back of a spoon, or spoon the meringue into a pastry bag and pipe over the grapefruit halves. Bake for 10 minutes or until light brown. Garnish each with a strawberry half and a mint leaf and serve immediately with grapefruit spoons.

Wild Mushroom Pie

John Fleer, Blackberry Farm, Walland, Tennessee

YIELD: 6 SERVINGS

3 Idaho potatoes, coarsely chopped
kosher salt to taste
$^1/_4$ cup heavy cream, heated
$^1/_4$ cup ($^1/_2$ stick) butter
freshly ground pepper to taste
3 ounces slab bacon, finely chopped
1 pound porcini, sliced
1 shallot, minced
1 teaspoon chopped fresh thyme
$1^1/_2$ teaspoons butter, melted
$^1/_4$ cup bread crumbs

Preheat the oven to 200 degrees. Cook the potatoes in boiling salted water in a saucepan until tender; drain. Spread the potatoes on a baking sheet and dry in the oven for 10 minutes. Increase the oven temperature to 375 to 400 degrees. Purée the hot potatoes, hot cream and $^1/_4$ cup butter through a food mill into a bowl and mix well. Season to taste with salt and pepper.

Render the bacon in a sauté pan until crisp. Drain $^1/_2$ of the bacon drippings from the pan. Add the mushrooms to the bacon and remaining drippings in the pan. Cook the mushrooms until lightly caramelized, stirring occasionally. Season to taste with salt and pepper. Stir in the shallot and thyme and cook until the shallot is tender, stirring frequently. Toss $1^1/_2$ teaspoons butter with the bread crumbs in a bowl until coated.

Grease six 2-inch metal baking rings with additional butter and arrange on a greased baking sheet. Spoon the potatoes into a pastry bag and pipe into the prepared rings until $^2/_3$ full. Top with the mushroom mixture and sprinkle with the bread crumb mixture. You may prepare to this point 4 to 6 hours in advance and store in the refrigerator. Bake for 10 minutes. Serve immediately.

COMPLIMENTS OF

Creamy Tasso Grits

John Fleer, Blackberry Farm, Walland, Tennessee

YIELD: 4 SERVINGS

3 tablespoons minced onion
1 tablespoon clarified butter
3 cups chicken stock
1 cup plus 2 tablespoons stone-ground grits
1 1/2 teaspoons salt
1/4 teaspoon pepper
1/4 cup milk
1/2 cup finely chopped tasso
1/2 cup finely chopped red bell pepper
1/2 cup finely chopped green bell pepper
1/2 cup minced green onions

Sweat the onion in the clarified butter in a saucepan. Stir in the stock and bring to a boil. Whisk in the grits, salt and pepper and return to a boil. Reduce the heat to low.

Simmer for 35 to 40 minutes or until the grits are tender, stirring occasionally and adding water if needed for the desired consistency. Stir in the milk and cook for 5 to 10 minutes longer, stirring occasionally.

Sauté the tasso in a sauté pan. Add the bell peppers and green onions and sauté just until the green onions are tender. Stir the tasso mixture into the grits and serve immediately.

Buttermilk Panna Cotta

John Fleer, Blackberry Farm, Walland, Tennessee

YIELD: 12 SERVINGS

1^1/$_2$ cups half-and-half
^{3}/4 cup sugar
2 vanilla beans, split and scraped
1 envelope unflavored gelatin
^{1}/4 cup water, at room temperature
2^1/4 cups buttermilk, at room temperature

Bring the half-and-half, sugar, vanilla pods and vanilla seeds to a simmer in a medium heavy saucepan. Remove from the heat and set aside. Sprinkle the gelatin over the water in a heatproof bowl and let stand for 5 minutes. Warm the gelatin mixture over a water bath until the gelatin dissolves.

Whisk the gelatin mixture and buttermilk into the half-and-half mixture and strain through a fine sieve into a metal bowl, discarding the solids. Place the bowl over ice and let stand until cool; do not allow the mixture to set.

Ladle the custard mixture into 12 small ramekins, dishes or Dixie cups. Chill for 1 hour. To serve, briefly dip the bottoms of the ramekins in warm water and invert into dessert bowls.

COMPLIMENTS OF

Chocolate Soufflé

Erling Jensen, Erling's Restaurant, Memphis, Tennessee

YIELD: 6 SERVINGS

granulated sugar for coating
7 ounces chocolate, chopped
3/4 cup (1 1/2 sticks) butter
7 egg whites
1/3 cup granulated sugar
7 egg yolks, beaten
confectioners' sugar or baking cocoa

Preheat the oven to 350 degrees. Spray 6 ramekins with nonstick cooking spray and coat with granulated sugar. Heat the chocolate and butter in a double boiler until blended, stirring occasionally. Remove from the heat.

Beat the egg whites in a mixing bowl until soft peaks form. Add 1/3 cup granulated sugar gradually, beating constantly until stiff peaks form. Add the egg yolks to the chocolate mixture and fold in the meringue.

Spoon or pipe the chocolate mixture into the prepared ramekins and arrange the ramekins on a baking sheet. Bake for 18 to 25 minutes or until the soufflés test done. Dust with confectioners' sugar or baking cocoa. Serve with crème anglaise or ice cream if desired.

Banana Cream Pie

Mac Edwards, McEwen's on Monroe, Memphis, Tennessee

YIELD: 8 SERVINGS

Banana Graham Crust

2¹/2 cups graham cracker
    crumbs
¹/3 cup sugar

¹/4 cup mashed banana
¹/4 cup (¹/2 stick) unsalted
    butter, melted

Banana Filling

¹/2 cup sugar
¹/3 cup cornstarch
¹/4 teaspoon salt
1¹/2 cups heavy cream
1¹/2 cups milk
3 egg yolks

¹/2 vanilla bean, split lengthwise
2 tablespoons unsalted butter
1 teaspoon vanilla extract
5 ripe bananas, cut into ¹/4-inch
    slices (about 1¹/2 pounds)
whipped cream

For the crust, combine the graham cracker crumbs, sugar and banana in a bowl and mix well. Add the butter and stir until moistened. Pat the crumb mixture over the bottom and up the side of a 10-inch pie plate and chill for 30 minutes. Preheat the oven to 350 degrees and bake for 15 minutes or until light brown. Let stand until cool.

For the filling, whisk the sugar, cornstarch and salt in a heavy saucepan. Add the heavy cream and milk gradually, whisking constantly until combined. Whisk in the egg yolks until blended. Scrape the seeds from the vanilla bean into the heavy cream mixture and add the pod.

Cook over medium-high heat for 6 minutes or until the custard comes to a boil and thickens, whisking constantly. Remove from the heat and whisk in the butter and vanilla extract. Discard the vanilla pod. Spoon the custard into a bowl and let stand for 1 hour or until cool, whisking occasionally. Stir the custard and spread 1 cup of the custard in the prepared pie plate. Layer with ¹/2 of the bananas and spread with 1 cup of the remaining custard, covering the bananas completely. Repeat the process with the remaining bananas and remaining custard. Chill for 8 to 24 hours or until the custard is set and the crust is slightly softened. Garnish with whipped cream.

COMPLIMENTS OF

EQUIVALENTS

CHEESE

4 ounces cheese = 1 cup shredded

CHOCOLATE

1 square chocolate = 4 tablespoons grated

1 (6-ounce) package chocolate chips = 1 cup

EGGS

2 egg yolks = 1 whole egg (for custards and sauces)

2 egg yolks plus 1 tablespoon water = 1 whole egg
   (for baking purposes)

FLOURS

1 pound all-purpose flour = 4 cups unsifted

1 pound cake flour = $4^{1}/_{2}$ cups unsifted

1 pound whole wheat flour = $3^{1}/_{2}$ cups unsifted

1 ounce flour = $^{1}/_{4}$ cup

1 cup self-rising flour = 1 cup flour plus 1 teaspoon
   baking powder and 1 teaspoon salt

FRUITS

1 medium lemon = 3 tablespoons juice

1 medium lemon = 1 tablespoon grated zest

1 medium lime = 2 tablespoons juice

1 medium lime = 1 teaspoon grated zest

1 orange = $^{1}/_{3}$ cup juice

1 orange = 2 tablespoons grated zest

MILK AND CREAM

1 cup whipping cream = 2 cups whipped cream

PASTA

1 cup uncooked medium noodles = 1 heaping cup
   cooked noodles

1 pound macaroni = 4 cups uncooked or 8 cups
   cooked macaroni

1 cup spaghetti = 2 cups cooked spaghetti

1 pound spaghetti = 8 to 10 cups cooked

7 ounces spaghetti = 4 cups cooked

RICE

1 cup uncooked converted long grain or wild rice =
   3 to 4 cups cooked rice

12 ounces brown rice = 2 cups uncooked or 8 cups
   cooked brown rice

SUGARS

1 pound confectioners' sugar = 4 cups unsifted

1 pound confectioners' sugar = $4^{1}/_{2}$ cups sifted

1 pound brown sugar = $2^{1}/_{4}$ cups firmly packed

VEGETABLES

1 medium bell pepper = 1 cup chopped

1 pound cabbage = 4 cups shredded

1 large onion = 1 cup chopped

MEASUREMENT EQUIVALENTS

8 ounces	1 cup
16 ounces	1 pound
2 cups	1 pint
2 pints	1 quart
1 quart	4 cups
4 quarts	1 gallon

MENUS

MENUS

COOKBOOK COMMITTEE

Heartfelt gratitude and appreciation are extended to the countless volunteers
who gave generously of their time, energy, and expertise.

CHAIRMAN
Mary Ann Stevenson

CO-CHAIRMEN
Mickey Schaffler   Nancy Edwards

RECIPE CHAIRMEN
Mickey Schaffler
Linda Woodmansee

RECIPE TEAM CAPTAINS
Sylvia Cochran
Pattie DePriest
Elaine Edwards
Ellen Fones
Mary Ann Gammill
Jean Gorham
Delaine Kelly
Pat Moran
Ginny Moss
Barbara Samuels

SECTION CHAIRMEN
Ann Clark Harris
Bobbie Lovelace

NON-RECIPE TEXT CHAIRMAN
Shirley Browne

NON-RECIPE TEXT COMMITTEE
Judy Belisomo
Cheryl Converse
Mary Alice Quinn
Suellyn Ruffin
Margaret Anne Taylor
Barbara Vincent

AD HOC COMMITTEE
Kathie Cavette
Arrena Cheek
Pat Comella
Ruth Dando
Linda Davidson
Sandra Eberle
Mary Elkin
Mary Lou Harkins
Marsha Hayes
Mimi McCracken
Katherine Mistilis, C.C.E.
Carole Pruett
Diana Teagarden

MARKETING CO-CHAIRMEN
Libby Aaron
Sandy Sherman

FINANCE CHAIRMAN
Carolyn Grizzard

PUBLICITY CHAIRMAN
Jean Gorham

SPECIAL EVENTS CHAIRMAN
Anne Piper

RETAIL SALES CHAIRMAN
Pat Moran

MARKET CO-CHAIRMEN
Bobbie Lovelace
Sylvia Cochran

WHOLESALE CO-CHAIRMEN
Ginny Moss
Susan Shindler

MARKETING COMMITTEE

Barbara Adams	Sue Dewald	Sally Greene	Jo Ann Ledbetter	Margaret Rankine
Barbara Albright	Elaine Edwards	Betty Harbison	Mary Leflar	Celia Ridley
Debbie Baker	Mary Elkin	Ann Clark Harris	Lola Llewellyn	Monta Robinson
Judy Belisomo	Carole Feisal	Anne Howdeshell	Mary Nelson	Nelse Sharer
Foy Coolidge	Mary Ann Gammill	Linda B. Jenkins	Helene Pepin	Barbara Walker
Linda Davidson	Virginia Gibson	Juanette Jones	Carole Pruett	Elise Wilson
Helen Dawson	Evelyn Gotten	Ann Lansden	Mary Alice Quinn	Dixie Wolbrecht
Pattie DePriest	Billie Jean Graham		Sue Ellen Rainey	Linda Woodmansee

RECIPE CONTRIBUTORS & TESTERS

Libby Aaron
Barbara Adams
Barbara Albright
Priscilla Alexander
Pat Dunlap Alsobrook
Betty Archer
Melinda Bagley
Carol Barnes
Ann Barton
Dale Barzizza
Judy Bechtel
Judy Belisomo
Jennifer Bermel
Willem Bermel
Berkeley Bettendorf
Barbara Billions
Anne Blackmon
Anne Boals
Teresa Bond
Gloria Bouknight
Judy Bouldien
Barney Bratten
Flora Bratten
Anne Broadfoot
Judy Brookfield
Anne Brown
Shirley Browne
Ann Byars
Betty Louise Caldwell
Kitty Cannon
Jeanne Cash
Kathie Cavette
Ginger Chapman
Mina Chase
Nancy Chase
Arrena Cheek
Patte Clement
Sylvia Cochran
Sally Coleman
Pat Comella
Foy Coolidge
Betty Cowles
Marilyn Crosby

Betty Cruzen
Ruth Dando
Linda Davidson
Helen Dawson
Christy Day
Pattie DePriest
Nancy Derr
Sue Dewald
Ann Dickey
Dawn Dillingham
Carolyn Dobson
Babs Ducklo
Carol Duke
Marilyn Eastin
Sandra Eberle
Elaine Edwards
Nancy Edwards
Mary Elkin
Jackie Falls
Carole Feisal
Pat Flinn
Ellen Fones
Mary Ann Gammill
Steve Gammill, M.D.
Emily Gay
Becky Geisewite
Peggy Geralds
Frankie Givens
Lynda S. Googe
Jean Gorham
Billie Jean Graham
Sally Greene
Carolyn Grizzard
Margaret Halle
Betty Hamsley
Jennifer Hanusovsky
Betty Harbison
Ann Clark Harris
Marsha Hayes
Carol Henderson
Kim Henley
Nancy Higgason
Lisa Holliday

Virginia Hollon
Mary Lillian Howard
Anne Howdeshell
Betty Jack
Linda Jenkins
Betty Lu Jones
Jean Jones
Sue Kaplan
Delaine Kelly
Nan Landess
Ann Lansden
Mary Leflar
Carol Lesmeister
Bobbie Lovelace
Jo Maxwell
Mimi McCracken
Mabel McNeill
Jenny Mealor
Vee Mechsner
Gail Mitchell
Beth Moore
Katie Moran
Pat Moran
Barbara Morris
Ginny Moss
Mary Mulherin
Mary Nelson
Ramona O'Shields
Dianne Papasan
Leslee Pascal
Maxine Patterson
Leslie Patton
Dorothy Pennepacker
Helene Pepin
Anne Piper
Geri Pitts
Chloee Poag
Danny Pooley
Audrey Pope
Carole Pruett
Tonya Rembert
Jenny Richardson
Jean Robinson

Monta Robinson
Pat Robinson
Barbara Samuels
Rita Satterfield
Jan Sawyers
Mickey Schaffler
Amy Shaw
Barbara Sherman
Sandy Sherman
Susan Shindler
Lavinia Skinner
Laura Oliver Spigener
Dorothy Spiotta
Eleanor Stevenson
Mary Ann Stevenson
Jane Stone
Margaret Taylor
Diane Taylor
Margaret Anne Taylor
Diana Teagarden
Mary Elizabeth Thomas
Carol Turner
Barbara Vincent
Barbara Walker
Jean Wall
Nelie Waller
Linda Walter
Cristina Ward
Mary Linda Wardlaw
Nancy Wells
Alexis West
Peggy Whitaker
Jean Ann Wiener
Elise Wilson
Joan Wojcik
Dixie Wolbrecht
Linda Woodmansee
Linda Work
Jolly Wright
Sydney Yarbrough

TRIBUTES & MEMORIALS

In Memory Of
Vivia Adams
Corinne Elkin
John Peyton
Frank Pierce
Fay Porter
Ann Clark Harris

In Memory Of
Lola Barton
Ann and Wilson Barton. Jr.

In Memory Of
Veda Pruett Beard
Anna Cox Pruett
William Pruett

In Honor Of
Our Grandchild
Taylor Dobson Bell
Carolyn and John Dobson, M.D.

In Memory Of
Dr. Howard Boone
Linda Walter

In Memory Of
Bobbie Buehl
Mike Isom
Rev. Turner Williams
Sally Pridgen

In Honor Of
Susan S. Burrow
Susan Dolan

In Memory Of
James A. Comella
Libby and Jackie Aaron
Carolyn and John Dobson, M.D.
Bobbie and Bill Lovelace
Mickey and Charlie Schaffler
Sandy and Phil Sherman, D.D.S.
Mary Ann and
*   Robin M. Stevenson, M.D.*
Linda and Bill Woodmansee

In Memory Of
James Coggin
Mary Jane Dotson

In Honor Of
The Cookbook Committee
Helene Pepin
Margaret Anne and Bill Taylor

In Honor Of
Foy Coolidge
Virginia Gibson
Kay Mistilis
Mary Ann Stevenson

In Honor Of
Betty Cruzen
Ann Clark Quinlen
The Wednesday
   Tearoom Shift
Ann Clark Harris

In Memory Of
Elena Signaigo Deming
Mickey and Charlie Schaffler

In Honor Of
Carolyn Dobson
Betsy Fox

In Memory Of
Maxine Skinner Driver
Merida Hamby
Gerald Horan
Geraldine Horan
Vera Long Horan
Carole Horan Pruett

In Honor Of
Our Grandchildren
Bailey Grace Elkin
Emma Corinne Elkin
Sarah Garner Elkin
Claire McDowell Elkin
Megan Daye Green
Brooks Meigs Green
Luke Thomas Green
Ella Daye Virostek
Mary and Tom Elkin, Ph.D.

In Honor Of
The English Tea Committee
Lunida Holland

In Memory Of
William L. Flinn
Mary Ann and
*   Robin M. Stevenson, M.D.*
Mickey and Charlie Schaffler

In Honor Of
The First and Third
   Tuesday Tearoom Shift
Cristina Ward

In Honor Of
Our Grandchildren
Dylan Craig Friend
Elizabeth Deane Friend
William Burton Friend
Susan and Buddy Shindler

In Honor Of
Jean Gorham
Sue Dewald
Mickey and Charlie Schaffler

In Honor Of
My Daughters
Kimberly Pruett Greene
Karen Pruett Norton
Patricia Pruett Parker
Carole Horan Pruett

In Honor Of
My Grandchildren
Clare Parker
Patrick Parker
Ryan Parker
Carole Horan Pruett

In honor Of
Sally Greene
Jan W. Sawyers

In Honor Of
Ann Clark Harris
Ann Clark Quinlen

In Memory Of
Bill Harris
Emily and Bob Walker

In Memory Of
Mary Elizabeth Herring
Madeline Owens
Ann and William T. Herring, M.D.

In Honor Of
Mary Lillian Howard
Barbara Pulsinelli
The 2004 Telephone Committee
Marsha and
Wayland J. Hayes, III, M.D.

In Honor Of
Ann Howdeshell
Sue Kaplan
Mary Ann Stevenson
Tonya Rembert

In Honor Of
Our Grandchildren
Erick Tucker Huseth
Jesse Hylton Huseth
Robert Corbitt Andrew Huseth
Lillian Avery Pascal
Michael Joseph Pascal
William Nicholas Pascal
Bobbie and Bill Lovelace

In Honor Of
Our Grandchildren
John Matthew Kakales
Mary Elizabeth Kakales
Betty and Charles Harbison, D.D.S.

In Memory Of
Mary Love Cox Kasselberg
Chloee K. Poag

In Memory Of
Doris Lake
Renee Clark Guibao

246

TRIBUTES & MEMORIALS

IN HONOR OF
Ann Lansden
Sue Dewald
Jean and Cliff Gorham
Denise Hinson

IN HONOR OF
Mimi McCracken
Mary Alice Quinn

IN MEMORY OF
Don Morgan
Libby and Jack Aaron
Marilyn and Bill Crosby
First and Third Thursday
  Tearoom Shift
Catherine and Adam Goode
Diana and Joe Teagarden

IN HONOR OF
Joan Morgan
Marilyn and Bill Crosby

IN HONOR OF
Barbara Morris
Carol and Al Henderson

IN HONOR OF
Marjorie C. Newman
Elaine and Tom Edwards

IN HONOR OF
Past Presidents and
Sustainers
Dixie Wolbrecht

IN HONOR OF
OUR GRANDCHILDREN
Carter Patikas
Sophia Patikas
Clyde Patton
Mallie Patton
Leslie and Clyde Patton

IN MEMORY OF
Thomas J. Pugh
Jean and Cliff Gorham
Mickey and Charlie Schaffler
Mary Ann and
  Robin M. Stevenson, M.D.

IN MEMORY OF
OUR BROTHER
Thomas Joseph (T.J.) Pugh
Bobbie and Bill Lovelace

IN MEMORY OF
MY PARENTS
Margaret and Yancey Quinn, Jr.
Mary Alice Quinn

IN MEMORY OF
Joyce Rasche,
Sewing Room Director
A Friend
Sally Pridgen
Mary Ann and
  Robin M. Stevenson, M.D.

IN HONOR OF
Mickey Schaffler
Jean and Cliff Gorham

IN MEMORY OF
Gladys Schlafer
Babs and Bob Ducklo, D.D.S.
Carolyn and Tom Grizzard, M.D.
Ann Clark Harris

IN HONOR OF
Pat Sexton
Virginia Moss
Grandsons: Blake Sexton,
James Sexton and
Parker Sexton

IN HONOR OF
My Wife Margaret
William W. Schaefer

IN HONOR OF
OUR GRANDCHILDREN
Brian August Schaffler
Jay Martin Schaffler
Laura Holland Schaffler
Mark Wilson Schaffler
Mickey and Charlie Schaffler

IN HONOR OF
Aileen Sharpe
Margaret A. Halle

IN HONOR OF
Nelse R. Sharer
Julie E. Thompson

IN MEMORY OF
OUR SON
R. Craig Shindler
Susan and Buddy Shindler

IN HONOR OF
Our Grandchildren
Olivia Ann Stevenson,
Mary Allyson Stevenson
Robin M. Stevenson, III
Mary Ann and
  Robin M. Stevenson, M.D.

IN MEMORY OF
Marcus Donlea Stevenson
Libby and Jackie Aaron
Dale Barzizza
Dr. Jeanne Stevenson-Moessner
Mickey and Charlie Schaffler
Sandy and Phil Sherman, D.D.S.
Mary Ann and
  Robin M. Stevenson, M.D.

IN MEMORY OF
Theresa Bervoets Sutherland
Granddaughters:
  Caroline Bervoets Sutherland,
  Emory Grace Sutherland and
  Robyn Ladd Sutherland
Arthur J. Sutherland, III, M.D.
Sutherland Cardiology Clinic

IN HONOR OF
Diane Taylor
Jean Robinson

IN MEMORY OF
HER MOTHER
Lucille Townsend Vare
Bonnie and Chapman Smith, M.D.

IN HONOR OF
Ann Wiseman
Barbara Adams

IN HONOR OF
The Woman's Exchange
  Cookbook
Barbara and George Albright
Barbara Ruth Chase
Carole and Victor Feisal
First Alliance Bank
Mary Lou Gaerig
Billie Jean Graham
Gail B. Herbert
Louise Householder
Betty Jack
Jane M. Mercer
Leo and Tom Meriwether, M.D.
Joan Morgan
Barbara and
  William Pulsinelli, M.D.
Patsy and Fred Roberts
Suellyn and Stan Ruffin
Pat and Jim Sexton, D.D.S.
The Head Turner Salon, Inc.
Blanche C. Thompson

NELSE R. THOMPSON

"I learned long ago that the word responsibility means the ability to respond. It is not a burden; it's a game, and I've enjoyed it thoroughly." Nelse's life was one of vision and service. Her involvement in The Woman's Exchange was in response to the desperate needs of women during the Depression. Over seven decades later, the Exchange continues to flourish. Your lifetime of helping has inspired so many to contribute their own talents. Thank you.

Elizabeth P. Greenway
Mr. and Mrs. George Lauder Greenway, II
Gilbert C. Greenway, III
Lilly Grierson Greenway
Nancy R. Greenway
Nelse L. Greenway
Mr. and Mrs. Daniel W. LeBlond
Lawrence Thompson LeBlond
Minor Banks LeBlond
Mr. and Mrs. Andrew McGehee
Mr. and Mrs. Thomas A. O'Connor
Thomas Andrew O'Connor, Jr.
Hugh Addison O'Dea
John Remsen Varick O'Dea
Patrick Gannon Greenway O'Dea
Sara Greenway O'Dea
Elizabeth Anne Peters
Ellen Blumeyer Peters
John Christopher Peters
John Reisinger Peters
Nelse Thompson Schreck
Mr. and Mrs. Frank Sharer

Anne Caldwell Thompson
Catharine Lawrence Thompson
John Shea Thompson
Julie Elizabeth Greenway Thompson
Mrs. L. M. Thompson, II
Lawrence K. Thompson
Mrs. Lawrence K. Thompson, Jr.
Mrs. Lawrence K. Thompson, III
Lisa Thompson
Mr. and Mrs. Martin F. Thompson
May Thompson
Sarah Thompson
Shea Thompson
Mr. and Mrs. Thomas Joseph Thompson
Thomas Joseph Thompson, Jr.
Valerie Rockwood Ellen Thompson
Mr. and Mrs. William R. Thompson
William Ryan Thompson
Katherine K. Winder
Nelse Tyler Winder
Mr. and Mrs. Jeremy Young

INDEX

INDEX

INDEX

INDEX

INDEX

INDEX

255

Compliments
—— OF ——

THE WOMAN'S EXCHANGE OF MEMPHIS

88 Racine Street

Memphis, Tennessee 38111

Phone (901) 327-2223 • Fax (901) 327-5672

Website www.womans-exchange.com

Name _____

Address _____

City _____ State _____ Zip _____

Telephone _____

Please send me _____ copies of *Compliments* OF at $29.95* each $ _____

Add 9.25% sales tax for Tennessee delivery $ _____

Postage and handling at $6.00 each $ _____

TOTAL $ _____

Method of Payment: [   ]   MasterCard   [   ]   VISA

                     [   ]   Check payable to The Woman's Exchange of Memphis, Inc.

Account Number _____ Expiration Date _____

Signature _____

*Note: Prices subject to change without notice.

Photocopies will be accepted.